# The Bible Survival Manual:

# Mystifying to Manageable

R F Pennington

Copyright 2012 by the author of this book, R F Pennington.
The book author retains sole copyright
to his contributions to this book.

Printed by Lightning Source Inc.
in the United States of America.

All Scripture quotations are from the New American
Standard Bible © 1975, Lockman Foundation. All
Greek Dictionary citings © 1981, Lockman Foundation.
Reproduction permission granted through Foundation Press
Publications, publisher for the Lockman Foundation.

This book published by BookCrafters,
Joe and Jan McDaniel. SAN 859-6352
bookcrafters@comcast.net

Copies of this book may be ordered at
www.bookcrafters.net
and other online bookstores.

ISBN - 13-978- 0-862-22-0

Library of Congress Control Number 2012917574

# Dedication

This endeavor is dedicated to anyone, anywhere, in any time zone of life who has taken the time to sit down and attempt to understand for themselves the Bible, the Word of God, and not only to understand it--but to be it. This book is further dedicated to anyone, anywhere, in any time zone of life who will follow in their footsteps and attempt the same.

Since you hold this book in one hand, and a Bible in the other, this book is dedicated to you.

# Table of Contents

Foreword..................................................................................1
Presuppositions.......................................................................6
Context is Everything...........................................................13
Conclusions............................................................................20
Understanding Your Bible's Origin...English-wise................26
Bible Readability...................................................................33
The Six Rules of Interpretation............................................41
Preparing for Bible Study.....................................................53
Propprecids............................................................................65
Reading the Bible..................................................................73
Further Hints for Effective Reading....................................87
Take a Breather!....................................................................95
Common Bible Threads......................................................100
Cranial Muscle......................................................................107
Hermeneutics........................................................................116
The Last Book......................................................................124
Final Thoughts.....................................................................128

# Foreword

Sometimes stuff gets dropped in our laps. Take this book for instance. I had been musing and rolling around the idea of a book centered on *how to study the Bible for regular folks* for several years now. Then, just about the moment I started fixin' to get ready to commence to write, I would look around at the myriads of books on this particular subject and wonder if I could justify the time, energy and funds to add yet another book to the pile, since it is a topic that has been worked, reworked for years if not decades. Actually, forever.

Then the impetus falls from the sky.

Actually, it didn't fall from the sky but came from the pulpit one Sunday in September, 2010 as I traveled back to Fort Worth, Texas to celebrate Grandmother's 103rd birthday. The whole gang clamored into the Heritage Church, where Brock Paulk delivered a sermon on *Sharing God's Grace as the Light of the World* starting with John 2:23. In that sermon he mentioned contemporary events in the Christian world of folks that claimed to be acting in accordance with the Bible--but were acting in a way that was anything but. Brock showed us a pastor wanting to publicly burn the Koran on 9/11. A second illustration was a small, yet frighteningly loud, Baptist church in Topeka, Kansas picketing the funerals of fallen soldiers in a hateful and judgmental way. This distressing list went on and on as Brock outlined that people today are still mis-using the Bible--and the name of Christ--to do hateful and damaging acts in the name of God.

That's when it hit me and I stopped dead cold--like you do when going barefoot through the yard and suddenly squish a slug between your toes. Do we really need another book on how to study the Bible? Evidently we do, as long as mankind is still doing nutty and hurtful things in the name of God, while hiding behind--and pushing--a twisted understanding of the Bible. The danger?--there are always a few, to some, to many who will buy their twist and follow them.

The next logical question in the sequence of queries is: what makes *me* the one qualified to write on this subject? Good question. If your answer would include the qualification of having ministered, preached or pastored in a large megachurch for a set amount of time, measured in years, with a couple-o'-thousand in televised attendance, alongside dozens of financially backed programs being carried out on a continuous basis, then I have failed in that arena. If your answer is along the lines of having a formal education in this area coupled with a couple of decades of teaching, preaching and writing about hermeneutics (herme-what-ics?--we'll get there), then I'm starting to fit the bill. If you add being an accomplished author, then I'm almost a bull's eye.

I remember hearing, somewhere along the way, the definition of being an *accomplished* author. [Here he goes!] One book makes one an author. When the second comes out on the shelves, it makes one an accomplished author. Three cement it. [Oh, brother!] Solomon said it is wearisome and endless. Whatever, but here you have it: a hopefully unbiased book for the common man in the pew who wants to make sense out of a Book that folks have been arguing over ever since the first collection was put together and the name *Bible* was stamped on it. Actually, there was quite an argument while they were putting it together.

We never seem to stop.

As far as approaches in this book are concerned, there are none--at least as far as slants. Hopefully, I didn't put any type of slant on this little work. By that I mean if you are looking for something that bolsters a millennial view or non-millennial view or an a-millennial view or an anti-millennial view of the Bible, then look elsewhere. If you are looking for a denominational approach or a non-denominational approach (whatever that is), then look elsewhere. If you are one of those sleuths who is always standing by with your decoder ring to grab and read the latest hidden message about Armageddon, then look elsewhere. Those are presuppositions that I'm simply going to bypass at this time. Presuppositions will get a bad rap later on in this book.

If you are desperately wanting to unlock the pages of a collective work known as the Bible so that you can learn to live a little more like Jesus would have you to live while stationed here on Planet Here, then this is the book for you. I don't claim to be an expert. No one is. I am simply one who has read, studied, read, listened, read, studied, and you get the pattern. Actually, if you ever find one who claims to be an expert on this or any other subject under the heading of Christianity then my only advice is to run just as fast as you can in the opposite direction. There was a group in the first century during Jesus' ministry that claimed to be experts. Jesus rarely had anything good to say either to, or about, these folks. Now let's get on with the study of the Bible, and how to do it.

In several places you will note that something is discussed two, even three, times strung across several chapters. No, I haven't lost my mind. No, my cutting and pasting didn't get out of hand. The reason for repetition is simple: importance! I want something on your mind before you hit such and such topic, then later we will detail the original something. I know, that sounds like fancy talk for a broken record but there is madness in that type of method...somewhere, I'm sure. I will hide behind Philippians 3:1 on that one.

One last thing I wish to share. I'm a bit of a clown, which I'm sure you are 'amen-ing' if you know me at all. I like to horse around, as it were, kidding and what not. Indeed, this backfired one Sunday morning with a visitor to our church building, who met up with one of our dear sisters. I could hear the sister beckoning the visitor to 'come and meet our Fearless Leader,' then, when she introduced me she added, "...and you can't believe a word he says, either!" Well, not a very stunning introduction for a Gospel Minister!

I guess I deserved that, but I wish to state that I've never been more deadly serious about anything in my life than I am about the subject of reading and studying and subsequent application of the Scriptures. As I will state elsewhere, God

The Bible Survival Manual:

may choose to talk to you in a dream, in a vision or even while you are seated in Red Lobster ready to order. That is his prerogative as God. One thing I know for certain about that is 1) it would be the exception, not the rule; and 2) He will never tell you ***anything*** (underline, *italics* & **bold!**) that is contrary to what He has already passed down to mankind--the Bible. Just not going to happen, folks.

OK, that was two things, but I'm certain of them. Now, here's the catch: if you DON'T know what the Bible teaches; if you DON'T know what God's Will would have you (as a member of the saved community known as the church) to do and be; if you DON'T know how you are to love your neighbor as yourself--because you haven't read, studied, understood and taken the Bible to heart--then you will not know if it is truly God giving you the dream or vision or talking to you while ordering fish and chips because you will not know if what is being related is contrary to Scripture or not.

I know far too many people who live and breathe for the exception, longing for that still small voice in Red Lobster. No, my friend, the rock solid foundation of discipleship and Christian living is found in the pages of your Bible. Nowhere else, no other book.

God has gone to great lengths to get that Bible you are holding onto shelves in the bookstore for you to read, study and live by. Men down through the ages have sweated and died to promote it, pass it around and preserve it. It is up to each one of us to spend a bit of time now and again to delve into its depths. You signed onto the roll call of the redeemed. Are you up to the task?

Please don't get disheartened while reading this book. Yes, there is a lot of stuff in here! Take it a little at a time if you need to. Most of us do that with things like cakes and a box full of moon pies. We don't sit down and try to scarf the whole thing down in one sitting (I said most of us), so why try to knock this book out in one weekend or across three evenings and call it good? If you have questions, make a note in the margin or on the inside of the back cover. Better yet, why not go ahead and invest in a Big Chief tablet? One will be required later on in this book, so might as well go ahead and procure one as we get started to get on with it! [At least he didn't do that seatbelt and hat thing]

Oh, and questions. We're always worried about stupid questions. The only stupid one is the one not asked. Well, OK, that doesn't work well during the Army's basic training. During basic, asking questions such as, "Why do we have to run all of the time?" or "Can we sleep in tomorrow?" are stupid questions. Drill Sergeant will impress that upon you. However, we're not in basic training for the United States Army. We're in a different army. Any question is a valid one.

Now, put on your seatbelt and hold on to your hat...

The Bible Survival Manual:

# Presuppositions

Well, now that I've gone through that little song and dance back in the foreword about not slanting and not giving in to our presuppositions, it may seem a little strange to title the first chapter in a Bible study book as **Presuppositions**. It seems strange because it *is* strange. I'm only doing it this way to keep this book in one volume. Let's face it, no one wants to read a trilogy on Bible study. Maybe one on Hobbits, but not Bible study. Besides, no one would buy it in the first place.

Perhaps I should call these, not presuppositions, but 'introductory thoughts' but the discerning reader would bust me anyway. There just isn't another word to safely use in this instance!

But before you drop this book and cry, "Well, here's just another opinion in a long line of opinions!" take a look at the following presuppositions. It is my belief that each of the following in the list will be borne out as being reliable as you move through this little work. If they aren't, then call me on it. I get emails and calls all the time with mistakes that I've put into print.

As a matter of fact, while writing this section I received a call from a dear sister who pointed out I made a mistake in one of my printed lessons on Balak, Baalam and the talking donkey. I had written in my Fifty-two Week Bible Study that Baalam's first and foremost mistake could be seen in Numbers 21:19. Well...it just can't! She was more than correct. Baalam's first and foremost mistake might be found in Numbers 22:19, but not in 21:19. I welcome criticism. Not harsh criticism, but nice criticism.

As Christians we should be nice, not harsh.

Yes, she was nice. That wasn't a hidden slam or anything. She's always nice, always. Her husband can get a bit grouchy at times, but she's always nice, always. We'll see her husband later on in this work but for now, let's look at another Christian couple found in the book of Acts of the Apostles.

Pricilla and her husband didn't brow beat Apollos and call him dimwitted and stupid in Acts chapter 18 in front of lots of disciples. Furthermore, they didn't act that way when they got him off to the side, either! My Bible presents a different storyline. We should keep that ever in mind as we go about holding Bible discussions or trying to teach someone out of an error or wrong belief they hold because of some faulty reasoning of the Scriptures. If not, we fall into the same category of folks that Brock Paulk was preaching *against* in the sermon mentioned in the foreword. I believe that sermon can still be listened to on the Heritage Church website, if interested. Let our speech always be with grace, just like the Apostle Paul told the church of God in Colossae along about chapter four verse six. Well now, I guess that was pretty much **Presupposition #1**. On with the list.

**Presupposition #2:** The Bible is the Word of God. Probably, if you are reading this book you believe that one, also. But let's take a minute and some space and allow me to flesh that one out, in case there is some reader out there hanging in the rafters. In stating that the Bible is the Word of God, I'm disallowing it being from the mind of man in its origin.

The Bible isn't something that the Jews sort of worked, reworked and added to over the centuries in order to codify some sort of theocracy. Actually, for crying out loud, why would they have wanted to do that anyway? The overwhelming majority of the Jewish leaders didn't believe Jesus when He was here. Why would they suddenly, after crucifying Him, decide to put together a book that was favorable to both Him and His cause, especially after He sprung back to life? But neither is the Bible faxed down from Heaven at the expense of individual writers.

What I mean by faxed down from Heaven is the erroneous belief that *every* word on *every* page is *exactly* how God wants it--that somehow God dipped into folk's brains as they sat in

The Bible Survival Manual:

a stupor, eyes rolled back into their sockets, and automatically wrote word for word stuff that was dictated from the throneroom of God. That is the short explanation, but it works for us at this time. It has worked for me for years.

Now, for sure, I've already stood some folks on their ears. I can hear the gasping all the way down here on the Mexican border! But let's take just a few examples, by way of questions, and see if this really holds up. Put on your seatbelt and let us commence: [Hey, Mister, we put it on at the end of the Foreword]

When Jesus, early in his ministry, got into a boat and landed on the eastern shore of Galilee, how many demon possessed folks did he run into? Mark chapter 5 tells me there was one. Matthew chapter 8 tells me there were two. Mark tells me that the one man spent his days in the mountains and among the tombs. Matthew tells me they mostly hung out along the main thoroughfare disrupting travel. Keep reading. One writer says that Jairus came up to Jesus and said, "My daughter has just died..." The other writer says that Jairus told Jesus, "My little girl is at the point of death..." and was only told of her death before the Master could get to her. So who is right?

If, indeed, these words were faxed down from Heaven in the *exact wording* that God wanted, then it would logically seem that God is somewhat confused as to the details! Yep, how many times have we heard that one from the naysayers?! Perhaps there is another explanation and that is the Bible writers were writing down things as they saw them (or heard them) with their backgrounds and understandings (or carefully searched out, such as Luke did) and that the Holy Spirit *did actually guide* them in this writing.

That would fall in line with what Jesus said to the apostles in John chapter 16 and what Peter wrote in Second Peter chapter first: the Holy Spirit of God *moving* and *guiding* men to speak and write.

I'm not so sure that Luke had even a clue that he was being somehow inspired by God to write a pretty hefty chunk of the New Testament when he told his friend, Theophilus, that he had researched out the story of the Christ and was putting it down on paper the way he heard and understood it. Read the first few verses of Luke. Just how did God do the moving and guiding as men wrote down these accounts of the life of Christ, Moses, the kings, the prophets and the apostles and writers sending letters to churches?

I don't have a clue.

And, let's face it, neither does anyone else, even though volumes of books have been written, hours of lectures at seminaries have been taught and a month of Sundays worth of sermons have been hammered from one pulpit after another pulpit! That, my dear Christian friend, is something that you can ask God when you get there where He is after leaving here.

Again, if you run into someone who has inspiration all figured out and prepackaged for your convenience, well, remember those running shoes I mentioned. For now, let's just take the presupposition that the Bible is the Word of God and it is in a form that seems to work for Him--and us--or it would be in a different form after all these years!

**Presupposition #3:** I am presupposing that the reader of this book is at least somewhat familiar with the Bible. Not a high powered bishop somewhere, just familiar with it. You understand there is an Old and a New Testament. You have read some of each. You have somewhat of a basic understanding of God creating the world, then mankind drifting away from God, Noah and the flood, Jews going into Egyptian slavery, the exodus and the receiving of the Big Ten at Sinai, populating the Promised Land, goofing up and going into Babylonian captivity but returning after seventy years, and finally, the coming of the Christ and the establishing of the church.

I'm also presupposing that if I write *Second Thessalonians 4:4*, that the reader knows where to go. Not a requirement that the reader can whing open their Bible to within a page or two of II Thess 4:4, but can recognize and find it--table of contents or not. Same will hold for Third Haggaliah 6:23!

And by being familiar with the Bible, I'm supposing that you are a believer in God. Not that I mind a stray atheist or two--or even one of them agnostics--reading my book, but much more will be gained from these pages if one is already a believer in God. One's faith may be small, confused, stunted or otherwise not all what it could be, but it is there. Hopefully, in some way, this book can help in the faith department.

Anyone can read the Bible anytime and figure out what God wants them to do, think or be. And, after all, isn't that what the whole point of God coming down here in the flesh was all about in the first place? He came so that the wall, the curtain, that separated man from God could be torn down in order that we could enjoy a one-on-one relationship with Him. Therefore, we don't need a Jewish priest to stand daily in the temple and offer sacrifices on our behalf. We also don't need a Minister, Pastor, Priest or Preacher standing <u>between</u> us and God telling us what to think, or better yet, *how* to think.

Beside us, helping us, yes. <u>Between</u> us and God, absolutely not! My Bible says there is One who stands between us and God while we remain on this earth. That One has been doing that job just fine over the last couple of millennia, ever since the stone was rolled away from the tomb and His life was triumphantly taken back. Yes, Jesus has the job. Anyone who would assume that position is a usurper, for it rightfully belongs to the Christ.

Take a quick gander at places like Matthew chapter 13 or Mark chapter 4 and simply scan for content. God in the flesh came down to earth to be one of us for a time, and to give us the mysteries of the universe and of life itself. He did it with...parables...stories about farming, fruit trees and food. He clearly tells us how to be and think, and how not to be and what not to think. In short, its not rocket science, it's eternal life! We are the ones who have muddied the waters about how many communion cups to use here, what to recite there, who marches into the Sunday morning crowd wearing what kind of garb holding this or that in their hand, when to kneel and when to stand, how much to give and to whom, who can say what and when and where. Jumpin' Jehoshaphat! No wonder the world laughs at us!

**Presupposition #5**: There aren't any hidden agendas or secret codes in the Bible. I wouldn't even give this any time if it weren't for the fact that this stuff just won't go away. MOST (meaning 99 & 44/100%) of the little coded ditties that folks seem to want to see here and there in Scripture won't hold up in another language besides English--never mind the fact that the Bible was written in Hebrew, Chaldee and Greek with a bit of Aramaic thrown in here and there!

The Bible ISN'T an English document. It was translated <u>into</u> English along the way, but also into German, Spanish, Italian, Outer Bogwanese and the list goes on. God sent His Word (somehow) down to man--and finally He Himself came as man about two-thirds the way through the writing of the Bible--in order to show folks the way to where He is. He didn't come down here to set up little coded messages hidden in the pages of the Bible so that a few fat cats could cipher it out like those cheap plastic decoding rings that we used to get in boxes of sugar saturated cold cereal. Let's not spend any time on this junk, shall we? Where's my antacids?

**Presupposition #6**: The Bible holds no contradictions. OK, easier said than done, but how many times have you seen or heard or believed something or other about this or that, only to have someone come along and throw in another related verse like the proverbial monkey wrench? Let's face it, this happens all the time, regardless of whether you believe you know the Bible 'backwards and frontwards.'

We will spend quite a bit of time when we get to the Rules of Interpretation on this one. Allow me to preview one of those rules for you, since it fits nicely right here with this presupposition: *difficult places in the Scriptures ought to be understood in the light of less difficult places*. In fact, the seeming contradiction may be cleared up with this thought.

The truth is that absolute truth comes only when all verses that pertain to any one subject are read and understood to the best of each one's ability. Let's start out pretty simple: you read one verse, Numbers 22:22, while studying Baalam and his talking donkey (this is the part where you might want to drag out a Bible and follow along) and you note that God is angry. Hmm. You hit your concordance and then find First Kings 11:9 and Psalm 60:1. Hmm. You conclude that God is <u>angry all the time with everyone</u>. Then someone comes up alongside and shows you First John 3:1. You have to revise

The Bible Survival Manual:

your thoughts on God, or continue in what would now be termed scholastic dishonesty.

I know, I know, that is *Introduction to Bible Study* (if not the first lesson in a child's Sunday school primer) but unless we do that *every time* with *every subject* the Bible has to offer, we run the risk of washing up on the wrong shore in our conclusions. First and foremost, we ought to limit our absolute, foot stomping conclusions from time to time knowing that we are a work in progress. Second, and just as important, we ought to keep an open mind that will allow us to change our conclusions when more information is gathered. I believe this last one is called spiritual growth. Too many disciples, including bunches of Pastors, Preachers, Priests, Scholars and Ministers, have allowed themselves to fall into this trap--and then remain there because of pride and a following.

Believe me, you don't want a following.

Have we lost the art of saying, "Idunno?" During our two years at Sunset International Bible Institute (*aka* Seminary, or Bible Boot Camp) while in our ten week, everyday, two hour stint in the Gospel of Mark, our instructor at the beginning of *every* class had each one of us stand up, look the other fellow in the eye, and say, "Idunno." Really grated on our nerves (especially when asked to do it at home in front of mirrors, wives, kids, the dog) because by that time we were darn near experts (sophomores!), but got us into the habit of being able to say, "Idunno" to others after we graduated and got frocked. I have had to say that about a gozillion times during my ministry: from the pulpit, over the phone, in a classroom, at retreats, through emails and snail mails. Don't be afraid to say it, even if you fall into the category of 'expert' --which if you break down the word 'expert' it comes from the Latin *ex* which is a *has been*, and a *spurt* which is a *drip under pressure*.

'Nuff on presuppositions. Let's go chase down some of the finer points of Bible study, our first stop being a most important item: context.

# Context is Everything

OK, I won't pull your leg with the Latin this time. Context comes from the Latin *con*, which means *with* and *texere*, which means to *weave*. Yup, weave together. But weave what together? Here's the answer: anything that needs to be weaved together to give the fullest understanding of what you just happen to be reading at the moment. Before we give some examples of pulling in the context of a Bible verse, let's take the time to explore a like-sounding, yet sinister word: *pretext*.

Just like the word *context*, the word *pretext* has a Latin base to it also. *Pre*, which means *coming before* is now coupled with *texere*, which means to weave. Yup, *weaving before*. But weaving before what? Before the story gets to be played out, that's what! Before the full meaning of what is intended is reached. So, remember this little ditty if you don't remember anything else out of this chapter or even this little book:

*If you take a **text** out of its **context**, you run the risk of making a **pretext**.*

I'm not sure where I got that little ditty, but a pretext is always a bad thing when it comes to Bible reading, studying and subsequent understanding and application. For a more enlightening definition, try this one for **pretext**: *a reason given in justification of a course of action that is not the real reason; an ostensible or professed purpose (i.e.) an excuse; an effort or strategy to conceal something.* Uck! Looks definitely like something to stay away from.

How many times do you pick up the paper or turn on the news and someone is saying something that someone else said except that the someone else didn't really say what

The Bible Survival Manual:

the first person said they said and you're saying to yourself, "Hey, they took that out of context!" In reality it was more than that, for they tried to create a pretext. Now, put yourself in God's place.

How many times a day do you think that God sits on His throne and listens to pulpit pounding Preachers and Pastors promulgating, postulating and pushing this or that and God says to Himself, or to some seraphim who might be hanging about, "Hey, they took that out of context!" I'll just bet you a dollar to a donut that it happens quite often. A verse here and a verse there, tweaked just a little in order to make it appear to say something that the Bible knows nothing about.

Sounds a bit like a certain serpent in a long ago garden.

Maybe this is a pretty good place to discuss just where these chapter and verse breaks came from. [I thought we were going to talk about garden snakes for crying out loud!] We do such a good job of throwing verses here and there at this person and that group (not so much chapters) that we need to stop and talk about the breaks. [Oh, OK, I see where he's heading] I don't know about you, but I really appreciate the chapter breaks. I'm not thinking that they are all that much needed in small entries such as Haggai and First John. I'm pretty sure that we could get through those books, even Obadiah :-), without too much trouble. I really appreciate the chapter breaks in Jeremiah and Acts (throw in Matthew and Hebrews, also). Seems that in the early thirteenth century an Archbishop and a Cardinal got together, as Cardinals and Archbishops are wont to do, and divided up the Bible into the chapters that are commonly in use today. And that's the story.

I like the chapter break study helps, even though they are not from God. I appreciate being able to stop reading in my Bible at home at the end of Isaiah chapter 22, and then go to a motel and pick up a Gideon Bible (you gotta love those folks) and start with Isaiah 23:1. But just think for a minute on the fact that God preserved the letter we call First John (or any of the sixty-six entries) with a flow and a thought, and never intended for us to throw around this chapter and that chapter--and the verse designations only make it worse. That was chapters, what about verses?

Verses were an invention of Robert Estienne in the mid-1500's. Some say that he partially divided chapters into verses while taking a rather lengthy horseback trip across Europe. If this is true, then I'm pretty sure that he was working on the first chapter of the Ephesian letter while riding on the roughest, cobble-iest part of the journey. Take a moment and look over Ephesians chapter one. Pick any translation you like that has verse breaks. Verse break after verse break in the middle of a sentence on both ends of the verse. Now, how is it that we get so dogmatic about what this verse says or what that verse says when it isn't even a whole sentence, let alone a whole thought! But we do. Now for a little exercise that will, hopefully, forever burn into your psyche the need for context. Consider the word **tear**. If you will, I will.

**Tear.** Now that might be a water droplet coming out of one's eye because of emotion or being poked, or it might be a rip, as in fabric or paper. Place an indefinite article in front of it: **a tear**. Not even a real sentence at this point, only a prepositional phrase. Add one more word to it: **a tear down**. I still can't tell if it is a rip or crying. Keep adding words, phrases, and even make a complete sentence out of it: **She has a tear down the front of her dress.** Yup, now it is a real sentence at this point, however, we still don't know if it is that she has a ripped dress or her crying has spilled over onto her clothing! Hmm, maybe both because of both.

And Christendom has gone to war over 'a tear!'

As we continue on with context, consider these verses that fall under the subject of soteriology (study of the doctrine of salvation):
- He who has believed and is baptized shall be *saved*
- Turn to Me and be *saved*
- If you confess with your mouth Jesus as Lord, and believe in your heart that God raised Him from the dead, you shall be *saved*
- The one who has endured to the end will be *saved*

The Bible Survival Manual:

- Your faith has *saved* you, go in peace
- And it shall be that everyone who calls upon the name of the Lord shall be *saved*
- Having now been justified by His blood, we shall be *saved*
- He shall speak words to you by which you will be *saved*, you and all your household
- The gospel which I preached to you, which also you received, in which also you stand, by which also you are *saved*
- It is with difficulty that the righteous is *saved*
- By grace you have been *saved*
- By grace you have been *saved* through faith
- And so, all Israel will be *saved*

Some of these verses you recognize. Some you may not recognize, or at least you're having to hit the concordance to find them. Some are complete sentences, some are just phrases (I pulled all periods and capitalized the first word on purpose!). There are many more such verses. Now for the questioning. Are we to pick one or two that fit into our thinking and explain away the rest? Is the way to God multiple choice?

Take a moment and look hard at the last two questions in the preceding paragraph. For too long mankind has answered 'yes' to both questions. Neither question can rightly be answered with an affirmative. Each time we do this, the entries under **Church** in the Yellow Pages grows longer. The problem is that the first and foremost item that is missing with the above bulleted items is context!

It seems almost incredible to witness disciples standing around discussing the finer points of theology and someone says, "Yes, but Isaiah 34:18 is crystal clear!" to which another will quickly add, "But, my dear friend, you have failed to consider Mark 10:53!" While Mr. Isaiah quoter is reeling, another will jump in there and state very emphatically, "You both need to read your Bibles a little more carefully. While both verses carry some merit, one cannot but include First Kings 17:25 in this discussion." From across the room, another yells over his shoulder, "Or you might try and read First Peter 3:23 once in a while, too!"

# Mystifying to Manageable

What!?

Even if those particular verses did exist (scramble, scramble), what is the point of tossing about a sentence or two, or usually just a piece of a sentence, from wildly differing entries out of the collection that we call the Bible? But, again, we do it all the time regardless of the context. It is time that the context once again takes its rightful place among the people of God. In your local church, its champion just might be you.

If you believe I'm overstating a lack of context, just listen carefully to many, many of the pulpiteers and television personalities make a statement, then rattle off a string, long or short, of verse references from the Bible. Happens much too often and it is dangerous ground to walk on. At first it seems way cool when they pull it off, however, it is anything but.

Let's finish out this section on context with another look-see into the Bible, this time from the book of Isaiah long about chapter 55 and verse 9 where it states: *For as the heavens are higher than the earth, so are My ways higher than your ways, and My thoughts than your thoughts.* That's it, case closed--and we have often taken that one verse by itself and place it upon ourselves in some sort of self-limiting way and conclude that we are not God (true) and, therefore, we just cannot rise above where we are (huh?) because God tells us we are lowly worms (what?) and we might as well just realize our place and go about our daily rat killing because He is in one place and we are in another on many levels (Oh, for Pete's sake!).

Now, go back and read the context. Look at it carefully and determine just how many verses in either direction you need to go in order to gain enough of the context to see what is *really* being said here. No, this isn't a trick. If I pulled an example from the book of Romans it would be a trick because the context starts in Romans 1:1 and finishes in Romans 15:33 followed by some notes. In this Isaiah passage, you need only go a few verses either way. What you will (hopefully) find is that God is saying, in effect, "My ways and thoughts are higher than mankind's. As My followers, you *should* take on My thoughts and ways..." Did you see it? If not, hit it again.

The Bible Survival Manual:

That is a far cry from using the verse to *separate* God and man. It is a verse, when taken in its context, that is calling mankind to emulate God's thoughts and ways. It is almost the gospel (meaning *good news*) both in a nutshell and in the Old Testament. It is the theme of the Bible as a whole. Context is everything!

This just might be the place to toss in the Case of the Bronzed Puppies since we are talking about verses in and out of their context. We should treat the Bible as a <u>piece</u> of writing, not something that is <u>in pieces</u> called verses. I've already mentioned that Ephesians chapter one has the worst verse breaks in the Bible, but it is nowhere the only place we could find. What if we were to take a letter written by Aunt Mabel, divide it into verses and then commence, around the dinner table that evening when the whole family was gathered to hear what Aunt Mabel had written, to discuss what she had to say in a verse-by-verse fashion? It might go something like this:

Verse 1: Dearest Nephew it was so good to see
Verse 2: Everyone doing well on our last trip
Verse 3: To see you will bring joy
Verse 4: Next time however this time she had
Verse 5: Puppies cost a fortune to bronze
Verse 6: Your baby shoes but will mail them soon

If we were to handle a verse-by-verse rendition of Aunt Mabel's letter it would sadly look like some of our adult Sunday school classes. We would be going on and on about how expensive it is to bronze puppies, whether we *should* be bronzing puppies, whether we should *dispense* with bronzing puppies--and give that money to the poor and homeless instead! We would only be going on and on about verse five because verse four would be hard to discuss and someone would venture to say, "Well, this is the most difficult verse out of the entire letter!" and we would all nod and say, "Amen, brother," and someone would lead a closing prayer and we would all go put our dishes in the sink.

Oh, for Pete's sake!

## Mystifying to Manageable

Wouldn't it just be a bit better to sit down and READ the letter from Aunt Mabel, putting in all of the inflections like we would *any other piece of literature* and the meaning might come out a bit different? Let's try this as a letter, shall we?

Dearest Nephew,
It was so good to see everyone doing well on our last trip to see you. Will bring Joy next time, however, this time she had puppies. Cost a fortune to bronze your baby shoes, but will mail them soon.

Instead of discussing the bronzing of small, just hatched dogs we could be discussing just what Aunt Mabel wanted us to know. We might even infer (or is that deduct?) that Joy is, herself, a dog and had pups to tend and couldn't make the trip, but that she would show up next time. Think about it. Which would you rather have? A verse-by-verse study of the Bible or a concept by concept study of the Bible? Me and mine? We're forever off the verse-by-verse trip, for it leaves us flat and uninformed.

As we leave this section on context, note that the next section builds, in part, on context. That is the recurring theme throughout the remainder of this work. Don't drop something just because the subject comes to a formal close and the page is turned.

The Bible Survival Manual:

# Conclusions

Once upon a time I had a television. Well, I guess I've always had a television but haven't had it hooked up to anything for the last seven or eight or so years. In my opinion (which means, in my opinion) there isn't anything to watch. Well, there are tons of commercials which account for about twenty minutes out of an hour's programming. There are also these really dumb thirty minute (meaning 19 min) sitcoms that insult my Christian intelligence. Don't get me started on some of the so-called news programs that twist and bend reality until I don't even recognize it. [Is he ranting?] I could care less about pawn shops in Casino Central, Dancing with Whomever and the kind of sports I like don't even get so much as a thirty second slot on any TV station.

During the times that I had a television actually hooked up to incoming, it seemed that the only time I did sit and watch something was in the middle of the night when I couldn't sleep--and that's when I couldn't find anything except these infomercials. Some of the infomercials caught my interest, especially this one that I tuned into right into the middle of the half hour (meaning 19 min) time slot.

The slick haired, smiling announcer stated: *So folks, it is as easy as pie. If you will just take to heart and put into practice all of those things that we have just talked about and have seen in action, then I guarantee that you will get the same results as all of these beautiful people you see on your TV screen right now!* And I looked, and there before me were a dozen or more multi-skin toned people all slim and trim and not a hair out of place, all with big white smiles--and holding these great big wads of cash in their hands.

I wanted to be them.

There was only one problem: seems that I landed right smack dab in the middle of this guy's conclusion! There was absolutely no way that I could figure out what he had said right up to the point that I tuned into his get happy/rich/trim ditty. I can't get rich off of a conclusion. I can't slim down on someone's closing remarks. I can only conclude when I have gone back and studied what he had to say to reach that conclusion.

So, I set my alarm for the next night and got up and was able to watch the entire infomercial. Yes, I know, all I had to do was send in a gozillion dollars and go irritate all my friends and neighbors, but you get my point. We cannot start with a conclusion. We can only understand or replicate the conclusion when we are armed with the points that led up to the conclusion.

But yet as disciples-at-large we seem to try to do it all the time when it comes to reading, reasoning and studying through God's Word, the Bible. Don't believe me? Consider the following words: *therefore, so that, to sum up, since then, for, and corresponding to that, so then, and in the same way, because of that,* or just simply the word *so*. In compiling this list of conclusion words and phrases I didn't have to go outside of two popular translations or even hardly leave the book of Romans!

Let's get down to the nitty gritty here. I wish I had a dime for every sermon or lesson I've heard (and, hopefully, never preached!) that began with Ephesians 4:1, "I, *therefore*, the prisoner of the Lord entreat you to walk in a manner worthy of the calling with which you have been called..." Now, that is certainly a worthwhile command that Paul laid out for the recipient church--and for us today--but we could just go everywhere throwing in this and that idea of walking in a worthy manner. The problem is, some have done just that. Wouldn't it just be better to back up in the Ephesian letter and see exactly what Paul was basing his conclusion on?

Someone might well say, "Well, then just switch translations to something that doesn't use the word 'therefore' and be done with it." OK, let's switch to another translation which tells me, "As a prisoner for the Lord, *then*, I urge you to live a life worthy of the calling you have received." Nice try, but the fact remains that Ephesians 4:1 and following--right down to the end of at least verse 13 if not all the way through verse 16--is a conclusion based on something that went on before chapter four opens up.

How about Romans 8:1: "Therefore, there is now no condemnation for those who are in Christ Jesus." That's a true statement, and a pretty strong one at that! There's even a traditional song sung nationwide by all flavors of churches that is word for word of this and the next verse. But the lack of condemnation for those who belong to Christ Jesus is based upon what? Can we just take that verse, and the promise contained therein, and just run with it applying it here and there? Well, we do it all the time but how about backing up to the 14th verse of the preceding chapter and looking at the struggle between the 'want to' and the sin that we always find ourselves falling into? It would certainly make a better lesson, and one that would be more likely to be on target!

Those who have listened to me preach, teach or otherwise lead a Bible discussion have heard me say a gozillion times, "Never, EVER, start a Bible study with the word *therefore* or any conclusion word. Back up! Back up! Back up!" Another ditty that will help you to remember to never start with a conclusion is the phrase, "*Therefore* is a conclusion of what went on *heretofore*."

Well, THAT was certainly catchy! I believe I can attribute that one to a certain Ed Wharton from my Bible Boot Camp days.

Someone once asked me not so much a question as it was a statement of conflict. She said, "Well, it's really, really hard to not start with a conclusion sometimes, because when you're doing a verse-by-verse study you just gotta start with a conclusion!" "Hmm, how about we dispense with the traditional verse-by-verse study," was my reply. She walked away in a manner that had a lot in common with the fellow in Mark 10:22. I had just rattled a long held tradition in many adult Sunday school classes and small group discussions.

Now, we are beginning to build on how to read and study the Bible. We need to remember that chapters and verses are man made helps, but can also be a distraction at times. We need to consider large blocks of Scripture in our reading so that the context can be set and the conclusions can actually

## Mystifying to Manageable

be based upon something and not just be stand alone entities. Let me give you another way in which conclusions, without knowing what they are based on, can trap the disciple of Christ in his reading of the Bible and subsequently his whole spiritual life.

Many of the churches that came out of the American Restoration Movement have latched onto a verse in Acts as almost a rallying cry of sorts. Yup, Acts 2:38--I just flushed a bunch of you out, didn't I? Now, for several reasons this verse is a very true, very telling verse. First and foremost because it is in the Bible, it is an answer to a question, and the weight of evidence for that one verse is overwhelming. To *not* believe that verse and what its implications are is to do an incredible amount of hermeneutical gymnastics and about a half a dozen other things that this book is, in part, trying to avoid. But Acts 2:38 is a conclusion nonetheless and is absolutely no place to start.

I remember one Sunday morning, during an adult Sunday school class, asking a series of onion peeling questions about that aforementioned verse. My first one was something like, "Is this a true statement?" to which everyone nodded their heads or otherwise affirmed that this was, indeed, so. My second was a question of why Peter said what he said to which I got the reply of, "Because of the question that people asked in verse 37!" You could see the faces on the Sunday school class begin to beam brightly, knowing that they were once again answering the time honored questions pertaining to Acts 2:38 correctly! Quite a bit of back slapping was going on, each participant congratulating the other for a job well done.

Peeling the onion back just a little further I asked then why the folks standing around Peter and the boys asked the question that they did--the question of what must they do. Folks immediately replied that it was because of the preaching of Peter on that first Pentecostal sermon. Faces glowed even more brightly at this point. Buttons began to pop off of shirts and blouses as folks squirmed and squealed with delight in their folding chairs. True enough answer, and upon my next question you could have heard a cricket burp among the four or five dozen folks that were busy staring blankly back at me: *Just what was it that Peter said?*

The Bible Survival Manual:

And no one knew.

No one could venture forth and tell me just what it was that Peter had to say concerning the Christ on that first evangelizing sermon. They couldn't tell me about the witness of the prophets or the witness of the miracles or anything. They had spent their whole lives putting forth and defending a single concluding verse and they had no clue as to why that verse was in the Bible (meaning why Peter said what he said).

I promptly rectified that situation, but have since noticed that this phenomenon has been repeated over and over. Not just with this verse, but with several places in the Bible. Instead of listing them, instead of writing out verses like First Peter 3:21, Galatians 4:7, Romans 10:13 and John 3:16 (the latter three even begin with the conclusion word 'for'), I'm going to ask that you personally find your concluding verses that you hold near and dear and often put forth in a Bible class or a small group discussion and make sure that you are not repeating this often made mistake. At least study out your time honored verses along with the context that leads the speaker or writer to come to that point. It will boost your Bible study and Bible knowledge by leaps and bounds. It really will.

Get started on that little exercise this coming morning between the hours of two and four o'clock in the morning when you don't have anything to do! In the meantime, we need to examine just where that Bible you are holding in your hand came from.

And I don't mean the Christian bookstore...

And I'm not talking about (OK, writing about...) who was inspired and when and under what circumstances. I'm not talking about scratching on parchment or vellum scrolls, then hiding the writings in caves for a few thousand years. As interesting a subject as that is, that is entirely a different subject than this little book. Again, I'm trying to avoid a multiple volume set right now.

When I mention origins in the next section, I'm intending the process of translation--turning the Bible from Hebrew scrolls and Greek letters on animal skins into English. I'm choosing English, because I'm making the presupposition (yikes!) that since you are reading this book, you are reading an English Bible! Let's go to Translation and Version Land, shall we?

The Bible Survival Manual:

# Understanding *Your* Bible's Origin...English-wise

Now the title looks like a no brainer. The answer is that it is the will of God for mankind. However, I'm not talking about the Prime Mover in this section, but talking about how did that book come from quills and parchment way back when, to being a leather bound collection in your hand in English-- and yes, how it got to the Christian bookstore. This is why the word *Your* in the title is italicized, for I'm speaking about the Bible you use which you currently (I hope) have in the other hand.

Again, this chapter isn't about who wrote what books and when, or even how it was preserved down through the ages. That's a whole nuther subject and book. I want to discuss *your* particular Bible. At this point, I'm going to make two statements that will help you decide whether or not you want to spend the time even reading this section.

The first statement is that this will not be an in-depth treatise on the very broad, very large subject. In order to remain a paperback book that doesn't cost a gozillion dollars it will have to be this way. The second statement is that you would be surprised at the number of folks that think the Bible was somehow *intended* to be in the order that it is in--and be in English! So, if you are an historical theologian, then you can skip this section. If you're just a plain old disciple, then carry on. There's some cool stuff in here!

So, for the inquisitive minds who are bummed over what this section isn't over, if you want to read something further on the subject of how we got the Bible--and can the manuscript be trusted--then as a starting point beg, borrow or steal a copy of F.F. Bruce's *The New Testament Documents: Are They Reliable?*

## Mystifying to Manageable

He has done a wonderful job in his little paperback book (complete, alas, with small print!) of leading the inquisitive mind into a knowledge of just how this book we call the Bible (focusing on New Testament reliability) came to be. However, let's go over some of the basics of translation at this time so that we can all be on the same page. To some, this may be an eye opener. Let's start with the word version. A version of the Bible is a specific translation.

Yes, yes, there is a difference--if one is on the scholar level--however, the difference is so small (again, since we are all reading this book--and I suppose your Bible--<u>in one language</u>: English) that we will, in this book, use the two terms interchangeably. We will get into the differing versions/translations a bit more in-depth in the next chapter, this is just the basics so we can keep rolling along.

Again, strictly speaking, there is a difference between versions and translations, but let's keep it *simple* since we're dealing with just one language: English! I have found over the last half century (or so:-) that simple works just fine most of the time.

Perhaps you have heard of the King James Version or the New International Version, usually shortened to simply the KJV and the NIV? These are both translated into English, yet they are two different versions. Over three-hundred and fifty years separates the *original* King James from the *original* New International Version (is the New NIV called the NNIV?). In the English language alone, there are dozens and dozens of versions spanning the last several hundred years. Each is unique for differing reasons. Some are targeted for young adults. Some are targeted for those who do scholarly work. Some are targeted for children. Some are more for reading than studying, while some are full of study helps, cross references and hefty indexes. All are useful and all can lead the reader towards the mind of God.

There is nothing more counterproductive, however, than the Wars of the Versions instigated and fought by Bible Battling Brethren. One person grabs a particular version because it is something that they can understand. Another person comes along and pronounces hogwash on that version because it isn't a 'word for word' translation like the one he (thinks he) is

# The Bible Survival Manual:

using. More on this waste-my-time battle in chapter next. The truth is, none of them are word for word translations because there isn't anyone in the English speaking world that would be able to understand it if it were written strictly in that manner. Driving back into Translation Land, let's take a fairly well known verse, John 3:16, and use it as an example as we travel from John's quill to your bookshelf.

The New Testament was written in Greek with a smattering of Aramaic and Hebrew words tossed in here and there. The Old Testament was written mostly in Hebrew, but let's concentrate on the NT right now. Not only was the New Testament written in Greek, but it was written in all capital letters (called uncials if you wish to be fancy), without any punctuation whatsoever or any spaces between the words. Yes, the book of John from our point of view was all one big long one-word sentence, just like Romans! So our example, John 3:16, looked like this in Greek:

ΟΥΤΩΣΓΑΡΗΓΑΠΗΣΕΝΟΘΕΟΣΤΟΝΚΟΣΜΟΝΩΤΤΟΝΥΙΟ
ΤΟΝΜΟΝΟΓΕΝΗΕΔΩΚΕΝΙΝΑΠΑΣΟΠΙΣΤΕΥΩΝΕΙΣΑΥΤΟΝ
ΜΗΑΠΟΛΗΤΑΙΑΛΛΕΧΗΖΩΗΝΑΙΩΝΙΟΝ

Did I get it right? Now, the English KJV (just because I had to pick one...) equivalent of all capital letters all scrunched up without any spaces or any punctuation would look a bit like this for John 3:16:

FORGODSOLOVEDTHEWORLDTHATHEGAVEHISONLY
BEGOTTENSONTHATWHOSOEVERBELIEVETHINHIM
SHOULDNOTPERISHBUTHAVEEVERLASTINGLIFE

Now, imagine the entire book of John just like that. So, as you can see we couldn't do anything with the above. It would drive the masses crazy and our Sunday schools would be out of control, that is, if we could get folks to come to Sunday school under those circumstances. Thankfully, someone back there in time decided to break up the original Greek text complete with lower case letters and some punctuation to help us common, everyday folks be able to read it in Greek. So we busted up the uncials, added some punctuation and some Greek breathing marks to help us pronounce it and it looked like this:

## Mystifying to Manageable

οὕτως γὰρ ἠγάπησεν ὁ θεὸς τὸν κόσμον, ὥστε τὸν υἱὸν τον μονογενῆ ἔδωκεν,
ἵνα πᾶς ὁ πιστεύωη εἰς αὐτὸν μὴ ἀπόληται ἀλλ ἔχη ζωὴν αἰώνιον

Now, all that might be clever and quite an undertaking, but it doesn't help the common person trying to sit down and read God's Word--at all! Now, let's revisit that rather pesky fellow that is always coming up to you and saying something like, "Well, you should get a REAL Bible, you know, one that is a 'word for word' translation..." OK, a word for word translation of John 3:16 from first century Greek into 21st century English would read this way:

*For such loved the god the world in order that the son the only begotten he gave in order that all the believing in him might not perish but might possess life-ages.*

Now I don't know about you, but I would get my fill of that in a pretty short while. Meanwhile, the adult Sunday school class is rioting again! But, for all of those folks that keep knocking your Bible translation, throw that one at them and see how they make do with it. In fact, that was so much fun let's take another pretty well known verse and do the *exact word for word* rendering out of the Greek:

*But the peter and even john they answering both said towards them if correct this is before the god you to hear rather besides the god decide all of you you for cannot for we things which we saw and even heard not us to speak.* Acts 4:19f

Well now, THAT ought to shut them up for a while!

Sadly, though, those that like to gripe and whine will always be given over to griping and whining. I know some folks, even if they were going to the gallows to be hanged by the neck until dead, would gripe if you hung them with a used rope!

So, back on track with this question of how we got our English Bibles that we are reading. This is it in a nutshell: rearrange the Greek from all capitals in order to make sense

The Bible Survival Manual:

out of it, then translate it into our language using the best words and phrases we have at our disposal. There are some that try to get closer to the 'word for word' end of things. The other end of the spectrum are the translations that tried to capture the phrases and intents of the passages (thereby, coming out with a different version!). Hang on, and we will return to a discussion of these fancy ideas I just tossed out in the next chapter in much greater detail.

Many moons ago, counted in decades, I heard from someone, somewhere, that the top reasons that people use the particular Bible they use is not for any great theological reasons, but for other reasons. Here are the reasons that were put forth:

1. The person grew up with this particular version
2. The person was presented with this particular version
3. All of the person's notes are in this particular version
4. The person knows his way around this particular version
5. Other versions just don't sound right (familiar) to the person

Now, I had picked my particular version out on purpose, and I had Great Theological Reasons for picking it. No one presented it to me. I presented it to myself quite some time before I even decided to attend, then subsequently set foot into, Bible Boot Camp to train for the ministry. In the little space where it says 'Presented to ___ By ___' I entered 'R F Pennington' and 'Self!' and then dated it. Stop me when I have my Bible and I will show you!

Needless to say, I didn't believe this fellow and his five reasons, but wrote the reasons down and tucked them away. What I have found over the years is that this person knew exactly what he was talking about (don't you hate that?). More often than not when I would ask a person what version of the Bible he or she used, the first thing a person would do is to close their Bible and look on the spine or flip real quick to the title page to see--because they had no earthly idea what version or translation they were using!

Any mistakes in any of the myriads of versions/translations out there? Plenty! Any mistakes big enough, monstrous enough, to keep the inquisitive seeker from drawing the right conslusion about God and winding up in Hell instead of Heaven? In a word: NO. Again: NO. So don't fall prey to the barkers and the naysayers who oppose this or that version and then push their favorite one. They're just barking and snorting and the serious child of God has better things to do than get into this kind of squabble. In the end, the problem with most disciples is not the particular Bible they use, but the fact that they do not use the Bible that they have!

Another one of my favorites is when the smarty pants deacon or pastor comes around and says, "Hey, that's a one man translation! That's just one man's opinion," complete with a bunch of arm waving and eyes all wide! Well, truth be told, all Scripture that has been translated into English is one man's opinion. There might have been quite a number of folks *on* the translating committee, but they didn't translate *as* a committee. Up to whole books of the Bible were translated by one person, then all the individuals threw in their sections of Scripture and called it good--then signed off as a group like it was the Declaration of Independence.

Bottom line is that all have mistakes. All are worthy. When I'm asked about which one to use, I might give pointers on readability (much, much more on readability later) and other factors but when all is said and done I tell them to try out quite a number before picking one for eternity. Again, we will revisit all of this section in more detail next chapter. It is that important to your Bible reading and study (two different things)!

And here's a little tidbit that I will throw in for free just for buying and reading this book: Always, always, ALWAYS, read out of as many translations as you can get your hands on. When this becomes practice, you will begin to appreciate the many benefits from diversity. You may have your favorite. I certainly have mine, but there may be a certain wording, a certain phrase in one particular translation that will bring an otherwise passive or obscure verse--and land it squarely into the lap of your life. You will spend many moments for many days thinking on that one verse because of it. You will come closer to king/prophet/shepherd David when he wrote, "I shall lift up my hands to your commandments, which I love. I will meditate on your statutes."

The Bible Survival Manual:

Besides, reading out of many different Bibles will help stamp out ninety-nine percent of those mistakes I said that all Bibles have. One version got a particular verse wrong, but two others you are reading got it right. Yes, weight of evidence is at play here. This will keep you from feeling you need to be a Greek and Hebrew scholar. I assure you, you don't need to be--just be a Bible reader and student.

Bible reading and studying can become addictive. If you are going to have an addiction, this is the one to have. As we jump into the next section, we will begin to flesh out all assertions that this chapter stated, so here we go...

# Bible Readability

Let's now expand a subject that would seem to be elementary, but I have found over the years that it is anything but. Let's continue with what we examined in the last chapter: moving the Bible from the original languages into your language so you can read it. In our example, we used English as the default language in question. Since there are several different versions in the English language, which one do we pick? They aren't all the same, so are some better, or easier, or less problems, or...I give up!

Let's take some time and talk about Bible readability, as the title suggests. The subject is a bit broader than most folks realize. Readability can be a physical phenomenon, or it can be textual. Let's tackle them all in our discussion.

There is a distinct event, a happening, that usually gives this first aspect of the discussion away: someone attempts to read out loud in a small group setting or Bible class. Everyone dutifully opens their Bible to the selected passage, while the person reading begins to strain and stumble over words too big for them to pronounce, let alone understand.

Other public readers strain, not at the actual words on the page but at the size of the words on the page! They move their arms back and forth trying to get the words into focus, all the while squinting their face into contortions that resemble being tortured. What's wrong with these two pictures? Bible readability in both cases! And since, as it turns out, this is the title of this section, let's give it a go, shall we?

The second illustration is easily dealt with either by purchasing a Bible with large print, growing a longer arm or getting your glasses fixed. Been there, done that, got reading glasses scattered all over the house (can't necessarily find them at any given moment, but they're here). Yes, it is easily

The Bible Survival Manual:

dealt with but I'm often surprised at the folks who tell me in conversation that they only get the large print books from the library, receive only large print magazines in the mail, yet they strain and struggle with a tiny print Bible week after year in Bible class. This assures me in many cases, through deductive reasoning, that they only attempt to read the Bible in class, also. That is a shame. That is not what God intended for us.

The first illustration is a bit harder to deal with. I am not a reading teacher nor am I a librarian. Neither am I an optometrist or a speech counselor. I do not deal with learning disabilities such as dyslexia and other phonological awareness and decoding shortfalls. What I am aware of is folks trying to read a book, any book, above their current reading ability. Here's where we can talk specifically about the different versions (translations) that are out there in Bible land. Although fast declining in popularity, because of mounting readability concerns, lettuce tackle a time honored translation.

Like many of the folks out there who are occupying a pew these days, I was brought up on the King James Bible. I've still got my first one. To this day, there are folks who use the 'King Jim' exclusively. If a person can read *and* understand the King Jim, then by all means keep using it. However, I never advocate using one version exclusively, regardless of what translation it is. More on that later, but first, a little rant.

What I will--and do--have trouble with was introduced to you in the preceding chapter. That is the person who states that the King Jim is the ONLY translation that should be used... period! This is usually followed by a folding of the arms, a 'humphing,' and the 'dare-stare.' They commence with all kinds of theological arguments stating blah, blah, blap about this and that stuff that don't hold water when you look at it. Actually, I believe this is the only version/translation out there in Translation Land where the beholders and champions actually hold to this type of thinking. Other translations have their supporters, but as far as I can tell the small sect of KJV'ers Only are unique in this approach. One would think that they were dying out, but in fact there are still quite a number--of all ages--of them out there, somewhere.

**Do Not Get Me Wrong Here.** Most everyone who uses a King Jim is NOT one of these rabid supporters of King James Only. Many, many folks who are older than me use the King James because they 'grew up with the KJV' and it is familiar to them (remember those five reasons?). I am saying that if and when you do find a 'my version only, or the highway' person, he or she is almost certainly holding a King Jim. Don't fret-- have fun! Let's take a little side trip.

If they really feel strongly about the King James Bible being the only Bible, then they shouldn't be using the 1760's revision (the one on the market--the one they're defending) or even the New King James Bible finished in 1982, but go way back to the real *authorized* version printed in 1611. Wait, authorized by whom or what?

English parliament. Wow, now *that's* a church heavy don't you know!

I assure you, there is no magical authorization from God. Just isn't, but back to the year 1611. One can now get their hands on a 1611 KJV from Zondervan Publishing as a 400th anniversary printing. Years ago I got to see an original 1611 KJV and spend some small amount of time with it (like, three minutes!) while wearing gloves. One thing is for certain: I couldn't read it with any speed or clarity. Word spellings have changed immensely (along with the shapes of some letters!) over the last four hundred years, not to mention the meanings! We don't use *spaketh* or *believeth* (my spell checker is shuddering!). First Timothy chapter one tells me that some *having swerved, have turned aside from unfeigned faith unto vain jangling* (1611: *hauing swarued, haue trundeth aside vnto vaine iangling*). I'm not sure what *vain jangling* is. Perhaps it is a rock n' roll band from the 60's that I missed somewhere along the way. All joking aside, you get my point.

There is more--much more--that can be said about the King James Only movement that would detract from what we are attempting to achieve here in this section of the book. There is even a Wiki article one could read if they are so inclined. I brought up this King Jim Only in order to identify it and give you, dear reader, something to run away from as fast as you can. *Authorized*

The Bible Survival Manual:

has nothing to do with God. The meaning and intent of that word *Authorized* got warped somewhere along the way.

In the last chapter **Understanding *Your* Bible's Origin... In English**, we were introduced to Dynamic- and Formal-Equivalence Bibles, though I didn't use those terms. These terms are not found in the Bible anywhere, nor in the concordance in the back of many Bibles. They are simply terms coined by Eugene Nida of the American Bible Society as a first-line division of the different translated versions. Let's hum a few bars and see how this tune goes.

Dynamic-Equivalence Bibles seek to capture the thought and flow of the original text and a Formal-Equivalence Bible seeks a more literal, word for word, translation of the text. That's pretty much it in a nutshell. Any problems with the two? Are you kidding?

Let's take the Dynamic-Equivalence first. What if I, as a translator, just happen to grab the wrong meaning from the original Greek or Hebrew or Aramaic phrase (or simply just one word) and write them down for you to read in what I believe the thought or phrase is intending? One can certainly see where that would ultimately lead the reader. I might grab that idiomatic phrase and wrongly turn it into an English idiomatic phrase, thereby missing the intended meaning. Now for the Formal-Equivalence Bible.

What if I translated the original language into a word for word copy (again, assuming I translate the word correctly!), yet what you are left with makes absolutely no sense whatsoever? Vain jangling, anyone? I take a Greek or Hebrew idiomatic phrase and translate it word for word and you are left with...nothing! There, in a nutshell, are the two problems. However, I also realize that this doesn't answer your burning question of exactly which type of Bible, D-E or F-E, you should sink your hard earned money into and read for the rest of your life.

Wait! Why are you thinking of sinking a bunch of money into a Bible? Believe you me, they can run extremely high in the price department. Why are you thinking you are sort of stuck with, or chained to, a certain Bible for the rest of your life?! See how we get as human beans? Why not spend a moderate amount of money on a couple of different Bibles that will span the whole spectrum of D-E and F-E? How about going cheap and getting paperback Bibles for a while. That would be the absolute best thing that you could do, especially since it segues into my next point: reading out of many different versions.

I'm going to stop here and count up what I have at home, in my car, and in my camper. I have two King Jameses, three New American Standards, two New International Versions, one Reina-Valera 1960, one Nuevo Versión International, two of The Message, one Revised Standard Version, one English Standard Version—no, make that two, one Version for the Deaf, one American Standard Version, one Nestle-Alland Greek New Testament and one NASB-Greek interlinear. In the 'just the New Testament cheap paperback' department I have a couple each of the NASB and NIV. Every one is marked in and dog-eared (Except my good, black NASB reserved for weddings and funerals!). What I don't have, I can hit the computer and get them online which isn't a bad place to test drive a version!

As a matter of habit I regularly read out of several versions. Suppose I wanted to read and study the book of James because it is the topic of both our Sunday morning get together and our Wednesday night get together and my Friday morning get together. I would first sit down and read James out of the New American Standard Bible (F-E) because it is MY Bible and then would get up and stretch and walk around (Thrown in for free just because. It isn't good to sit for too long, especially as you get older). Next, after refilling my cup of coffee, I would read out of the New International Version (D-E). Later in the day I would read James out of Eugene Peterson's Message (an extended D-E, sort of a D-E on steroids) and the next day I would read James from the English Standard Version (F-E). Finally, I would find time to read out of the New Living Translation online, which is a sort of an F-E/D-E compromise.

Now, I know what some of you are already thinking after reading that last sentence: "Hey, why not just pick up a copy of the NLT, since it is a mix of the two, and be done with it?!" Well, stop thinking that and re-read the last paragraph over again in its entirety. Overall point was missed.

Yes, most (but not all, by far) of my *study* (I described *reading* above) will be out of the NASB, but I purposefully read

The Bible Survival Manual:

out of different versions which fall in differing camps. We all at this point know why: I might catch something out of the Message that I didn't get from the ESV, or the ESV might have been a bit unclear on a word, but the NIV hit it on the head.

I am also heading off the first possibility--at least narrowing it--of getting something wrong because I didn't explore all of the possibilities of the other versions. Next, I am heading off the second possibility of becoming stuck in a rut. And for the first--but not last--time, a rut is a coffin with both ends kicked out. Coffins are for dead folks. You let God's Word bring you to, and keep you in, life.

So, there you are, ready to read and study the letter from James and you are sitting in your comfy chair and surrounded by a whole stack of Bibles spanning the D-E/F-E spectrum. You pick up the first one, an NASB, and start reading, "James, a bond-servant of God and of the Lord Jesus Christ, to the twelve tribes who are dispersed abroad, greetings."

The only problem is, you stumbled over the hyphenated *bond-servant* and have not a slap-clue what one is. Then, you marveled over *twelve tribes* and couldn't pronounce *dispersed* in your head (kept coming up with *dispensed*) and all the while you were doubly glad you weren't reading out loud to some Sunday school class! Here's the problem in a nutshell: you are attempting to read over your head.

I'm not saying nuttin' here, except you are reading over your head! Remember the nice lady we met at the front of the book? Her husband (Mr. Sometimes Grouchy) is a very good friend, a dear brother in Christ, who is as spiritual as anyone I will meet here on this side of the Jordan river. He's also way older than me, but that's not important. He doesn't believe it, but he understands more about God and the church than a gob of stuffed preachers and pastors I know. Folks listen to him and value his opinion on matters. Here's something else about him: he can't read worth squat.

Curiously, he's very good with the stock market, but not in the reading market.

He has much in common with Mike whom we will meet a bit later in this book. He will pick up--not an NASB like two paragraphs back, but--the World Bible's Easy-to-Read Version (*aka* Version for the Deaf) and begin, "From James, a servant of God and of the Lord Jesus Christ. To all of God's people who are scattered everywhere in the world: greetings." More often than not, he will simply listen to Scripture on CD, or his wife reading to him, rather than waste his energy on the physical aspect of reading. Good enough, wouldn't you say?

Yes, it is. If that is what it takes to get God's Word into your ears, down the pike and into your brain, then that is what it takes. There is absolutely nothing gained by beating one's head into a brick wall with something that is too tough. Nothing gained.

All of the above illustrations and stories are to attempt to get everyone to grab a hold of a Bible that they can read and understand and not waste precious and valuable time trying to bridle a dead cat. If you can't read well, then get a Bible you can read. If you can read well, then get a Bible you can read without stumbling over the shortened sentences. There are many, many Bibles out there. Test drive before you buy. Keep many at hand.

To-date, the Bible has been translated into nearly five hundred languages. If you take the New Testament only, then the number soars into the thousands. In English, there are nearly one hundred translations that one can still get their hands on in bookstores, so there stands to reason that there must be one or two or three out there that you can read *and* understand! If that fails, then get the Bible on CD. Put it into your *iPhone* and listen on the way to and from work or while on that treadmill. If you don't have a CD player or a fancy phone, then spend a few bucks and get someone to come over and read it to you every night while you are tucked into your bed!

Do Something!

Again, the Bible has been preserved for you. God went to a lot of trouble (and so did a few folks here and there!) in that preservation. He expects you to read it and take it to heart. It is, flatly, His Will for your life. You must take the initiative to

The Bible Survival Manual:

get it off the pages and into your life. It ain't gonna come no other way.

In the meantime, don't waste even a precious moment of your life listening to, or arguing with, someone who has a version agenda! There is nothing more counter productive than the Wars of the Versions, unless you are batting for the other team. Satan likes us to bicker and argue. If it takes standing on a mountain top holding your left foot, hopping up and down while reciting nursery rhymes to get a Bible you can read and understand, then go do it. It is that important!

# The Six Rules of Interpretation

OK, now a third of the way through this book here it is, the stuff you have been waiting for--as human beans we like LISTS! And, as it turns out, so do I. Many will read through this section and say, "Now, this is why I bought this book!" You might also wonder why I didn't just put this on a page or two and post it on my weekly website and be done with it. Mostly because I obviously like to write books and you like to read books, so let's get on with it shall we?

It would seem that interpretation is really the heart of the matter. Without interpretation, the Bible is just so many words on a written page. Without interpretation, we don't have any chance at application. And let's face it, application is the name of the game: how to go from being like us to being like God. Now here, as we talk about interpretation, we're ceasing to talk about the translators interpreting the Bible during the ciphering process from Greek and Hebrew to your tongue. We're talking about each of us individually interpreting some portion of Scripture and placing it into our lives.

Some of these main points we have already talked about, at least a little bit. It is in this section that we will begin to put workable items into play. If you find these handy, you might consider finding one of those blank pages in the Bible (all Bibles have them somewhere) and writing them down with either some of the chapter and verse examples or some that you have found along the way or will find after reading this section.

And take it slow. It might have burned down in one day, but Rome wasn't built in that short of a time period. Take the time to look at the Scripture notations and see if it makes sense. If need be, make another pass at it before you pronounce done on this book and relegate it to the yard sale or recycle bin. On to the rules.

The Bible Survival Manual:

## 1. Identify in the passage who is speaking and who is being spoken to.

Men's locker rooms are a place where one has to watch it, and watch it closely. While in a men's locker room one must look manly, walk manly and above all watch what one says while in the locker room. I don't know about girl's locker rooms. I haven't seen inside one since the eighth grade. Got expelled for it.

Now, imagine that as you are drying off from the shower and other guys are tying shoes or popping each other with towels, there are two men engaging in a conversation over to your left. No, your other left. One holds his hands up (actually one hand up and the other holding his towel around his waist) and says, rather excitedly, to the other, "I really love you!"

The locker room will come to a dead halt with a <u>very</u> dead silence. All eyes and ears will be on the one who just gave his undying love to another similarly scantily dressed individual. It is then when the center of everyone's attention (rather quickly) goes into the explanation. "Oh, hey guys, I was just telling my boy here what my girl said to me last night when we went out on a date. It's all cool, all good!" OK, either the guy was telling the truth or he thought fast on his feet, but either way if he had not identified who was REALLY speaking and who was REALLY being spoken to, we would have all come away with a different conclusion.

But sometimes in our Bible studies, Bible classes, small groups or just our individual study time--because we have bad habits of grabbing verses here and there--we don't have a CLUE who is speaking and who is being spoken to. It gets worse when we get into some of the prophets in the Old Testament.

It may be as easy as Exodus 7:8 where we read, "Now the Lord spoke to Moses and Aaron, saying..." That's pretty cut and dried. Even the village idiot can understand that what is following is something that God Almighty told Amram's two boys.

We are forever going to be locked into chapters and verses. What if we were studying the Parables, or stories, of Jesus and

## Mystifying to Manageable

someone started with Luke 14:16: "But he said to him..."? With just those five words, one cannot tell ANYTHING about who said what to who (or is that whom?). Now, if you are on top of your game and paying attention in Sunday school you just might get off lucky with guessing that the 'he' in the verse is Jesus, since Jesus is the one that usually gives parables in the Bible (but not always!). However, you wouldn't have so much as a clue who the 'him' is without backing up a few verses and seeing who is hanging about in that particular setting.

One may have to pay close, very close, attention to who is speaking and who is being spoken to when you get into the Old Testament prophets--the land of *he* and *him!* There are times when it is a rough ride. Sometimes we just need to be reminded that the person speaking isn't speaking directly to us. Here's where the hot water starts running.

I am very aware that the Bible is a book that was written, preserved, collected, ordered, printed, bound and finally sold to us by a bookstore so that we can understand the mind and the will of God *for us in our lives* and then ultimately die and go to Heaven. However, we need to think critically at times and understand that everything which is promised directly to someone in the Bible is not particularly promised to us.

Sometimes it is. Take Peter's preaching in Acts chapter 2 on Pentecost, ten days after Jesus ascended back to the Father. As we saw earlier in our discussion on Acts chapter 2, the crowds asked a question in verse 37. Peter answered the question in verse 38. Does that hold true for us as well today? Well, Peter seemed to think so in verse 39. Take the time to read those verses and see how that works.

Go back and examine the teachings of Jesus in Matthew, Mark, Luke or John as He spoke to the crowds, multitudes, followers or whatever your translation says. Jesus laid out generalities for all mankind and didn't put a time limit on it. For instance when He gave the parable of the wise and foolish builders He said, in effect, "Those who listen to My words and put them into their lives will be like wise builders..." Same is true today, just as it was two thousand years ago. If we listen (by way of reading) and heed the teachings, we will be blessed.

Sometimes, Jesus was speaking to a few folks and had

some specific things to tell them or even to promise them. Some such verse can be found in John 14:26. I don't know about you, but I've heard some say (and teach) that we really don't need to study or read the Bible because the Holy Spirit of God will give us what we need to know. I've even heard some Pastors and Preachers try to live by this 'promise'--and it shows in their "I got nothing worthwhile to say" sermons and furthermore in their lives!

I'm sorry, go back and look at that section of Scripture. Who is speaking and who is being spoken to? Is it open for all people at all times? No, it is specifically given to the apostles. Besides, look at the verse real careful like. I'm not sure about you, but I'm not old enough to have had Jesus say something specifically/physically to me. I'm not talking about euphemisms and church talk, I'm talking about having the Lord stand there physically and tell me something while I'm trying to repair the dishwasher, reload pistol ammunition, or clean the windows on my truck. In this verse, this section, Jesus is talking to the apostles and giving them a promise that seems to have been carried out in Acts chapters 2, 3, 4,...Galatians 1:11*f*...you get the idea.

Again, as in many of these illustrations and examples given, these will just be one or two of, perhaps, many examples found in the pages of your Bible.

## 2. The reader should take care and identify the circumstances or factors in the surrounding textual context that will affect the understanding, significance, outcome and subsequent application of a particular passage.

[Holy cow! What did that guy just say!?] OK, my bad, let's just put that into plain English: *'nuther words, what's going on in the story?* This includes context, yes, but stretches a bit farther out than that.

When I was growing up, I forever heard about the unforgivable sin. If you grew up hanging about church buildings at all and you are my age or older, you heard about the unforgivable sin, also. Not only did we hear about it but we also were given certain definitions as to just what that sin might be. Once, and I don't know exactly where or from whom I heard this, but I heard that the unforgivable sin was taking the Lord's name 'in vain' just like it says not to in places like Exodus chapter 20 and Deuteronomy chapter 5. Even king David ratted out some of his enemies to God in Psalm 139 for doing this very thing.

So far, so good (or so it would seem...keep reading), except that I didn't have a clue what taking the name of the Lord 'in vain' was specifically--then I was given a definition. I know now that it is an utterly wrong definition with absolutely no biblical support whatsoever, but I was just a kid. The definition? Using a certain combination of words in a swearing fashion that I had heard countless dads use out in the neighborhood when they hit their finger with a hammer or discovered that their kids had been in their toolboxes, tackle-boxes, or they had simply run out of beer, or some such crimes.

Wouldn't you know it, not too much time passed before I hit my finger with a hammer or some kid pushed me down or whatever and I spouted that same set of words in response. My syllogistic deductive and inductive reasoning kicked in and I came up with the fact that I had committed the unpardonable (unforgivable) sin. At that point, what's the use in even 'going to church' anymore since I was damned to Hell already? But I was a kid.

What about adults that get fed this line of hooey, followed by the reading of passages such as Mark 3:28-29? After reading those two verses *by themselves without any context whatsoever* it is easy to see that folks can be told (read: by the ones with the robes, collars and three piece suits standing behind the pulpit) all kinds of things, right or wrong, about this passage and set panic and guilt in rather quickly. Stuff like this is always followed by a passing of the offering plate, but that is a different story. When we reach a pretty heavy hitting passage such as this one, what is needed is context-- lots of context!

Mark 3:30--the very next verse--states clearly, "Because they were saying, 'He has an unclean spirit.'" Important? Quite so, for Jesus had just given the teaching--*and meaning*-- of the unforgivable (unpardonable) sin! For another example, John 6:15 goes a long way in explaining the story found in that chapter. Without that verse explaining Jesus' actions, we might be tempted to think Jesus was attempting to stay aloof from the crowds or some other nonsense.

## 3. Notice if the language is meant to be understood literally or figuratively.

Isaiah chapter 11 begins: "Then a shoot will spring from the stem of Jesse, and a branch from his roots will bear fruit. And the Spirit of the Lord will rest on Him, The spirit of wisdom and understanding, The spirit of counsel and strength." This is understood to be figurative for the Messiah. No one would take this literally, not even those who profess to take the entire Bible in that manner. Is there someone out there who actually believes that Jesse was going to grow a green shoot of some type of biological plant matter out of his...roots?! If so, I definitely want to hear from you!

However, in other places in Scripture, we fail to make this distinction, with disastrous results: "They are spirits of demons… to gather them together for the war of the great day of God, the Almighty. And they gathered them together to the place which in Hebrew is called Armageddon."

Let's consider some more figurative language. Our everyday language is peppered with idiomatic phrases. Peppered!--see what I mean? One inquires of Farmer John, only to be told that he 'kicked the bucket' a few days back. Everyone sighs, except for someone who speaks English as a second language. They're wondering what bucket, what the bucket did that ticked the farmer off, how far he kicked it, how big was the guilty bucket...and has no idea why everyone is taking up a collection for Farmer John's family! An idiom is only one of many types of figures of speech. Metonymy, sibilance and alliteration (especially in the Psalms...along with some anaphora!), hyperboles, synecdochical and tautological phrases (of which Paul loved the latter) are but a scant few of the many figures of speech found in the whole of the Bible.

Jesus used superlatives and hyperboles quite often (camels going through the eye of a needle) when He spoke to crowds large and groups small. This list can go on and on, but one has to be *very careful* when they take the rigid stance that the Bible is a literal piece of literature from Genesis to Concordance! Nothing is further from the truth. The faster the reader of the Bible can understand this, the clearer some of the teachings will become, Old or New Testament.

This can't be stressed enough.

Let's consider an animal on which the Bible clearly gives us information, if not a bit of instruction. I recently watched a science documentary that contained a rather lengthy discussion about a pelagic lampriform creature known as the oarfish. We don't harbor a great amount of knowledge about these rarely seen fish. Indeed, most of what we know, we know from examining dead or dying specimens washed up on the beach.

This is seemingly in stark contrast to James 3:7--*For every species of beasts and birds, of reptiles and creatures of the sea, is tamed and has been tamed by the human race*--which clearly tells me that we have already put the bit and harness to these animals, inclusive of the oarfish--unless one understands the concept of figures of speech. Don't worry, if you didn't readily grasp my little oarfish side trip. You probably will about two o'clock in the morning when it hits you and you sit straight up in your bed hollering, "Oarfish!" On to number four of the Rules of Interpretation.

**4. Partial truth on any one subject is only able to direct one to a conclusion. Full understanding and truth comes about when all the verses that pertain to a subject are read and considered.**

John said, "God is love." Ethan said, "God is faithful." God said, "I am jealous." Moses said, "God is angry." David said, "God is compassionate." Peter said, "God is patient." God said, "I hate them." Get the picture? Indeed, if one only has (or examines!) First Corinthians 14:34 concerning women…

What the Bible student should understand--and always keep at his fingertips--is that what they may be reading in Mark, or Hebrews or Genesis just might not be the place where

The Bible Survival Manual:

all the truth on that particular subject would fit. Allow me a Bible illustration.

Someone, for instance, may have asked the Master, or Peter, or someone a question concerning salvation. The answer *that was needed for that person at that time* may only need to consist of a few lines covering only a small aspect of that very large subject. Remember our discussion of whether or not salvation was multiple choice? Let's tie that in with everyday life.

I ask you why my car isn't running correctly. You look at it and state that all four tires are flat, looks like someone cut them with a knife, and I need to get four new tires put on. That isn't the time and place for you to instruct me in the total maintenance of my vehicle: oil changes, spark plug gap setting, checking the timing belt and flushing the radiator! Actually, come to think about it, I really, really need an oil change. Hang on and I'll be right back.

OK, that's done. Sorry, and thanks for waiting. Now, if the Bible were simply a manual faxed down from God with subject headings and chapter entries, such as soteriology and eschatology, with a cross referencing index in the back, then that would be a different subject. However, this isn't what the Bible is. Yes, some of my brothers treat it like it was a Chilton's Automotive Manual, but it isn't. Don't make it one!

The Bible is a collection of five and a half-dozen individual entries that range from predictive prophecies, personal letters, history, biographical accounts, poetry and congregational directives in the form of letters. We will expand this one out completely a little later in the book. God intended mankind to read--and wrestle--with the contents of this great book.

## 5. The difficult passages ought to be understood in a way that harmonizes with less difficult passages. The Bible holds no contradictions.

We touched on this one when we were discussing the presuppositions, but we will now dive into this one a bit deeper. Let's start with an example from the first letter Paul wrote to Timothy:

Paul wrote that women will be preserved through child bearing at the end of chapter two. We have two choices: 1) teach that women should have lots of kids in order to go to Heaven, or 2) teach that women and men alike go to Heaven because of the saving grace of God. They are mutually exclusive doctrines. The latter is harmonious with the bulk of the Bible. I have spent many years trying to figure out what Paul meant about women and child bearing. I have examined all of the arguments and found each one of them severely lacking in one or more areas. I haven't got so much as a clue what he was talking about there. I do, however, understand fully the doctrine of salvation by grace through faith.

Until I live out my life here on earth and God finally calls me home to the other side of the Jordan River, I will have to keep the 'child bearing' passage in the 'Idunno' category, for I believe the Bible holds no contradictions. I guess I will just have to ask Paul what was up when he wrote that little bit of the Bible. If you get there before me, don't be hanging out at the gate waiting to tell me. Let me find out for myself.

Actually, Paul has probably been asked that question so many times now, he probably has some explanation posted to the door of his room. I would, if I were him!

Now, this is a good time to raise the question as to what makes a passage difficult? I'm going to get pretty bold and to the point on this one: often times, WE do. WE are the ones who make the passage difficult. How can this be? What is it that WE do that could possibly make a passage travel from the understandable to the non-understandable category...and then remain there? Allow me to toss out a couple of reasons...

A passage is asking us to do something that is against our human nature and desires. Not evil desires and the really horrible things we are capable of doing to each other. Nothing such as murder, rape and pillaging, just passages that ask us to do something against human nature. I'm thinking more along the lines of not gossiping, lying (yes, the little whities), window shopping with regards to the opposite sex, things like that. All of a sudden, all the passages that tell us that these are no-no's suddenly become 'hard.' Along these lines, as we continue, passages that tell us to be living sacrifices or to pick up our individual crosses daily or give first of ourselves then our money, become muddled and arguable points for the simple fact that we really don't want to surrender self and be

The Bible Survival Manual:

wholly placed under the Master's disposal, let alone cut loose of our hard earned cash. Think about it.

Another reason is the reason of Party Line. I held off as long as I could, but cannot any longer. Every group has these pesky little lines in the sand. Every denomination clings to and touts them. I don't care if you tout yourself and your organization as 'non-denominational' you are still denominational, and that is the first of your pesky sand-lines! Creeds can be written or unwritten, but they are powerful indeed. Creeds, manuals and such just simply do not match up with the Word of God one hundred percent (at times even 'mostly') and when the two are laid out side by side for comparison, we begin to waffle between the two and then--due to peer pressure and fear from the Party--start proclaiming loudly, "This verse is, perhaps, the hardest verse in the Bible to understand..." This list can go on, but let's get on with it. I often feel like I will someday have a stroke when it comes to creeds and manuals.

There are, however, hard passages. Some are hard because the language is obscure with an idiom tossed in, like the women birthing lots of babies for the sake of salvation. Some are hard because we haven't yet read and understood all there is to understand about that particular subject. We may not yet have anything to hang that teaching or concept on. For instance on the last, let us consider the statement 'Husband, love your wives...'This will have very little meaning to some fellow who isn't married. He may think he gets it, but he doesn't really. Not yet. Up to that point he may have loved a girlfriend, parents, a dog, a rifle or a movie--but this fellow hasn't struggled with a marriage bond for years and decades.

Ho'boy, is that fellow ever in for a surprise!

One promise concerning hard passages that you can take to the bank: if we never devote the time and energy and really dig deep and read and read and study a passage out, it will certainly never come to us by way of a correct, working answer. If we simply stay child-like in our approach to Scripture and never tackle a certain subject, the true meaning, and subsequent application, will stay far, far away from us.

Over the years, I have been taken to task on the last sentence of the preceding paragraph. Folks have been quick to bring to my attention the statement that Jesus made in Matthew 19:14 or even 18:3-4. I understand what Jesus was telling the listeners. I'm thinking more along the lines of what the Hebrew writer was penning forth in the beginning of chapter five and spilling over into the beginning of chapter six: get going on the road to spiritual understanding and maturity! In a large part, this is what this little book is intending to assist one with!

## 6. The student of the Bible ought to possess an open mind free from prejudice, opinions or preconceived ideas.

Read Second Kings 5:1-14. Note in the story that Naaman states, "Behold I thought," however, he thought <u>wrong</u>. He was prejudiced, opinionated and was weighted down with preconceived notions. If we are the above, we will be wrong--just as he was. We all create a box over time, especially if we become too comfortable and quit challenging ourselves in regards to Scripture. We must learn to think outside of that box or find ourselves in a rut. Keep ever in your mind that a rut is simply a coffin with both ends kicked out.

For the time being, I will leave this sixth Rule of Interpretation alone. A little further along in this book we will spend quite a bit of time on **Propprecids**, where we will return to this sixth rule, but need to discuss preparing to study the Bible first. Presuppositions have already been dealt with earlier in the book. We will have the presupps, but ought to drag them out, dust them off from time to time, and check them against God's Word.

Keep in mind these six rules, copying the rules into one of those blank pages in the front or back of your Bible if that will help. Many, many mistakes in interpretation can be traced back to breaking one or more of these rules, thereby rerouting the true meaning of a passage or verse into the dangerous realm of isogesis. Isogesis (which we will also discuss further down the line) breeds weirdness, and there is too much weird Christianity out there these days for my taste. How about yours?

The Bible Survival Manual:

In fact, weird Christianity is what is keeping folks away from our church buildings (therefore, away from the folks sitting in those buildings and, sadly, away from God and His grace) and we should do what we can to curb it when and where possible. Just a thought, perhaps a goal.

# Preparing for Bible Study

While writing the lion's share of this book, I went and hid myself in the wilderness for a couple of weeks. OK, not really the wilderness but down in Big Bend National Park just me and my camper. I had to borrow a battery operated computer from my wife so that I could recharge with solar power [How did he do that?]. I had to load the software onto her computer that I was using to create this book. That was the easy part. I had to go to the grocery store and buy fourteen days worth of mostly canned chili with beans and some Spam so that I wouldn't starve to death while typing. I know fasting is a Bible topic, but I've never really gotten the hang of it.

Food wasn't the only item on the list. Due to some clown driving his vehicle into mine at an astronomical rate of speed, I had to get a new vehicle after being released from the hospital--and then have a hitch installed. [Is there a point?]

The point I'm trying to make is that I had to PREPARE to go on this little trip. We prepare all the time in life, though we might call it different things. We 'get ready' in the morning to go to work or school. We 'make lists' before we go to the grocery store, or at least I do so I don't come home with duplicate pork chops or add a dozen eggs to an already dozen and a half at home. If you are still in the realm of dating then you really begin to appreciate the concept of preparation.

Rest assured, your date appreciates it, also.

So why do we attempt to do serious Bible study without any preparation at all? I'm reminded of the lady that told me she just simply sat down and opened up her Bible every day and wherever it opened and her finger landed was where--

The Bible Survival Manual:

and what--God wanted her to read--and do--for that day. Her attempts at the Scriptures were no deeper than that. She asked me what I thought, so I told her what I thought.

To begin with, I told her that God wanted her to read ALL of the book, that's why He had it bound in such nice leather. [Did you really tell her that?!] I then asked her where she got her personal information about what God wanted and how He wanted her to read. She mused and humphed a bit on that one.

Then, I asked her to open her Bible to Second Kings chapter six and read the story about the floating axe head and then asked, "Suppose you opened up to that place in your Bible. The chapter starts midway down the first column on the left hand page. How do you know where to start? (She started with whole chapters---but see discussion on chapters and verses again if you need to) How far do you read? (Only one chapter at the most, unless it was a long one, then a few verses) Now read it and tell me what God intends for you to take home from this chapter and accomplish today?"

Good brethrens and sisters, you know where this is going and, indeed, where it went. She read the chapter and said, "Well, that's a cute story!" That was the sum total of God speaking to her that day.

I'm not going to get into a discussion on whether or not God speaks to you personally or how He carries that out. If He wanted to speak to you--or me--personally, He is God and that's well within His realm and power to do. This must remain a Bible Study book. I do know one way in which God speaks to every person in every time zone down the years and centuries and that is through His Will for mankind we call the Bible. It is half of what we call communication. Let's take a minute and go back over this thing we call the Cycle of Communication with God.

We talk, God listens. That is called prayer. God talks, we listen. That is what we call Bible reading or Bible study. Put those two together and you have effective two-way communication. Just like sitting down over a cup of tea and talking to Aunt Mabel about having her puppies bronzed. She talks while you listen, then you talk while she listens. Anything else is not communication.

## Mystifying to Manageable

If Aunt Mabel just blab, blab, blapped all the time and wouldn't let you get a word in edgewise, that would be called dictation (among other things) but not communication. But, hopefully, you are starting to get the picture. If all we do is pray, pray, pray and never let God get a Word in edgewise, then there is no effective communication, for we are simply dictating to God. If we have a cycle of prayer, reading, prayer, reading, then an Effective Cycle of Communication is in place. This was the concept, if not almost the exact words, I ended my third book with. It is important enough for me to bring it, once again, round for everyone's attention. So how does this fit into preparation for our Bible time?

Easy! Talk to God about what you are reading or fixin' to read. Hmm, after all He IS the author of what you are about to read so why not ask Him to open your mind, open the eyes of your heart, give you understanding, whatever or however you wish to call the intended result. Remember, I said to ask the Author.

I always got tickled when someone would come by my office at the church building where I ministered and ask to borrow a book. Not just any book, but a commentary. They would say something like, "I have to teach a lesson next Sunday from Luke chapter five and I was wondering if you had any good books on the subject?"

"Well, as a matter of fact I do!" I would say as I reached for an extra Bible on my shelf. They would look at me as if I had lost my mind, say something like, "Um, I already got one of these..." and hand it back to me and then shoot a longing glance over toward my collection of commentaries I used to own.

I would share with them what I have already shared with you in the preceding couple of pages. More often than not, they would not return to my office--not because they particularly thought I was a loose cannon, but were convinced. All I'm asking is that you ask the God of the universe to help you in your study and understanding of the Scriptures. I can't stress this enough.

Now, think back on the beginning of this section. Try to make a mental note of all the things in this life that you prepare for, whether it is the daily grind of getting out of bed and going off to your designated rat killing, or the longer preparations

The Bible Survival Manual:

such as college or preparing your children to one day leave the house and go out on their own.

After you have gone down your own personal list, then think about the all important journey that you will one day take from here to eternity. Yep, it comes one per customer! Shouldn't we put as much preparation into this journey as we do the others? If, indeed, the totality of preparing for the afterlife consists of showing up at some church building on Sunday morning for an hour, participating in the automatic rote exercises for that same hour, and finally dropping money into a plate to pay for that hour, then prayer, study--including this book--are true time wasters. I'm just willing to bet you don't believe that--at all. I really, really hope you don't! Besides prayer, there are other items that we can attend to in order to complete our realm of preparation. One comes in the form of questions.

You will have them if you delve at all into the depths of the pages of the Bible. They will start with the usual *who, what, when, where, why* and *how* words (henceforth known as the *who-whats*). This is where you will need that Big Chief tablet and a sharp pencil we spoke about way back at the front of this book. When you have them, the procedure is simple: write the *who-whats* down!

That may seem like a no-brainer, writing down the *who-whats*, unless you are like me and your memory isn't what it (supposedly) used to be. That is *yet another reason* why I make a list before I go to the grocery store. It is only a mile from the house, but I just get inside and obtain a shopping cart that has four good wheels and suddenly I'm standing in the middle of the store with a dumber than dumb look on my face and store people are asking me if I need help. Yes, I need help all right, but not the kind that they're thinking of! So, write your questions down. And what do you do with the *who-whats* once their written down? [If he says, 'get an answer,' I'm gonna scream!]

Here are some Don'ts, and let's start with the biggest one: don't go running to the pastor, priest, preacher or anyone else with 'all the answers.' You will, sadly, simply get their opinion or their understanding of the answer. That's not what you want. You want to develop your understanding of the answer, not become a little carbon copy of the fellow in the pulpit. This is where you--like Hezekiah laying out his problem before the Lord--lay your question out to the Lord and ask Him for an answer. Then listen when that answer comes.

How, or when, will it come? Here's where I pull out the 'Idunno' answer that I had to practice so many times while standing in front of the family dog, but I'll toss in some possibilities. It may come to you that afternoon. It may come at you crystal clear the next time you sit down to read further into God's Word. It may come in next Sunday's sermon at your particular church. Yep, I just said it may come from the Preacher. It may come in a discussion with other brothers and sisters in a mid-week Bible class. I don't know--maybe in a Chinese fortune cookie! All I'm trying to get across is to ask God and then give Him time to get back to you.

We have lost the art of waiting--especially waiting upon the Lord.

We live in a fast paced world where we can simply Wiki some question and then have it answered in less than the time it takes you to read one page in this book. There is something to this being still and knowing that God is God concept. If we always run to the head knocker at our church and get all our answers from that head knocker, then we become little mini-knockers! I'm not knocking knockers. I are one from time to time. But I do believe that the Bible holds truths and greatness for everyone. And it can be understood by everyone, yes it can.

And don't try to do the end run play with your question. What I mean is, don't try to say, "Well, I'm just going to see the Priest anyway about some unrelated matter, so I might as well get a commentary from him that will answer this burning question..." Nope. Again, a commentary is an opinion and you will simply answer your question with someone else's answer. You ask God and let Him get back to you on it. I have seen this concept work time and time again.

Again, we have lost the art of waiting--especially waiting upon the Lord.

The Bible Survival Manual:

So, let's see what we have in this section so far: ask God to bless your time in His Word, then write down any questions you may have and give them to God and wait for the answer. Do you see a pattern here? I hope so. And I do hope that you don't get the sense that I'm trying to steer you away from your Pastor, Priest or Preacher. If they are honest and good folk who have honestly studied the Word of God to some degree of depth, they are a great source for information on many aspects of our lives. I am trying to help you develop good study habits that will unlock the treasures that the Bible holds for anyone in any time in history on any continent.

Did I mention reading? What I mean by reading the Bible is actually sitting down and reading the Bible. Not the 'thought for the day' off of some calendar or the daily liturgy thingy from your church bulletin in preparation for the next Sunday's homily. By reading I mean sitting down with your Bible with the television off, radio in the same position, and reading it like you would a book from the library. Here's where different types of Bibles come in handy. Not translations here (another place in this book for that), but in the way the Bible is laid out.

Some Bibles were made for reading. Some were made for studying. Let's tackle the latter first. Those made for studying have all kinds of insertions and color coded texts in the margins. It has a habit of pulling your eyes away from the text and into the side trips. This can be a distraction. In fact while I am typing this I am sitting in a place down in the Big Bend called Dugout Wells, a sort of oasis in the Chihuahuan Desert. I can't quite see them, but there is a small herd of javalina fighting in the bushes about fifteen meters behind me. I've gotten up twice to go hobble off and see what all of the fuss is about. Each time I get near, I can hear them gallop off into the underbrush but they come back and start all over. One of them smells bad. Maybe the others are trying to persuade the smelly one to go wash it off! See what I mean about distractions?

There are types of Bibles that are made for reading--just reading! There are no margin notes. There are no color coded ditties spaced here and there. No concordance for those of you who can't resist peeking in the back to look something up. Some, like The Message, have dispensed with the verse breaks within the text and have put them at the top of the page. If you are used to reading a verse or two, then running to the margin notes to see what all of the fuss is about, then this type of actual reading I'm describing is going to take some work, real work. Or, one can do what Mike did.

Mike was a grown man, father of a few. Mike had a full time job and a mortgage. One thing Mike didn't have, that most of us have, is the ability to read. Severe reading problems, but Mike had two good ears on either side of a pretty good brain. Solution? Bible on tape, however, Mike didn't have the money to buy any tapes. While in seminary, I was required to read the entire Bible many times. Therefore, I would read the Bible out loud and record it for Mike. Problem solved.

Of course, now it is Bible on CD or iPhone, but you get the gist. Even if you can read, and read well, this is an avenue that you might explore especially if you are one that cannot help but run to the concordance every five or so words!

There have been vast improvements over the years by folks who put the Bible on listening media. It has grown from one person reading the text (inserting chapter and verse numbers as they came--all in a droning monotonic delivery) to great productions with sound effects in the background, with several gender-specific actors reading the various parts when it comes to dialogue. I strongly recommend this avenue while driving, walking, treadmilling at the local gym or even vegging in the back yard, but back to reading.

I don't want to overstate something that I went over in-depth in other books, but I believe that this example is worth repeating. While taking a class on the Book of James, we were required to read James once before class (each time out of a different translation from the previous day). Class was every day for ten weeks. Whatever particular chapter we were studying from at the time, someone read it out loud at the beginning of each class. You do the math, but at the end of the semester every one of us K-N-E-W what was in James. We not only knew what was in James, but could tell you that some particular word was on the left hand page, inside column and about two-thirds of the way down!

I still can, and several decades have passed.

The Bible Survival Manual:

There are two kinds of people in the world. There are those who are visual and those who, sadly, aren't. Me? I'm visual (and I hope you are, too). If I read about Jesus calming the storm in Mark or the scattering at the Tower of Babel in Genesis, I can see it. Add a little audio in there, also: I can hear Baalam's donkey talking. One other item that has helped me in my reading of the Bible are the books that tell me about the times and customs of Bible times. Now, THAT is a long, long period.

I know, there are some of you that are secretly saying, "Aha! I've got him, that rascal! That's a commentary because I've got a set of commentaries and that's the last (or first) book in the set: *The Life and Times of Bible Lands*, or *Customs of Bible Times*." OK, you *sorta* got me, but not really. What I mean about commentaries, however, is someone commenting on what a particular verse (usually) or passage *means* and *how to apply it.* Think of a 'Life & Times' book as a para-commentary of background material. And they can be useful, very useful.

There was a vast difference (by bunches of hundreds of years) between the folks in the Mesopotamian world during Abraham's time and the Jewish customs under Roman occupation during the times of the Gospel accounts. Sure, I guess everyone ran around in robes and had long beards (usually, just the men) and rode donkeys, but there is a vast difference between Noah, Isaac, Ethan and Alexander the coppersmith. Books like these can help you not only plug yourself into the times and seasons of that particular point in time, but can help you *unplug* yourself from *your* present day surroundings. Aha!-we just found something else that is important: unplugging yourself from your present day surroundings!

This one little overlooked item can get us into a real stew and we aren't even aware of it. For instance, Jesus tells a little story found in Matthew chapter 13 about a man who was crossing a field that was obviously not his, and found a treasure. He hid that treasure and then went and bought that field. If we are not plugged into the New Testament times and culture--and not *unplugged* from ours--we will sit all afternoon wondering why this person was trespassing in the first place!

We will wonder, "Why on earth would Jesus use someone who is breaking the law to illustrate the Kingdom of God?"

There are many times and customs that were understood at the time of writing that may be lost to us now without a little elbow grease. For instance, turn in your Bible to Luke chapter two. Read verses 21 and 22. You know from the reading of verse 21 that Jesus was eight days old when He was circumcised. The next question is: how old was Jesus when verse 22 took place? Was it that same afternoon? Was it early the next week?

Without an understanding of the customs and times (or a reading of Leviticus chapter 12), you would not know that Jesus was about six weeks old when verse 22--and the subsequent blessings and prophecies by Simeon and Anna--took place. Now, I know it isn't the difference between Heaven and Hell if one does not know this, but information like this makes the Bible come alive and is a type of preparation for reading and studying the Bible that all of us can do. It does give us some insight into the type of folks Joseph and Mary were, young as they were at the time.

They were so dedicated to carrying out the various sacrifices that the Law of Moses required in regards to childbirth that they were willing to stay in and around Jerusalem (Bethlehem was only a few miles south of the capital) to carry these out instead of packing up the new fam and heading home way, way up north. When Luke was writing, he pretty much understood that his recipient, Theophilus, would have an understanding of Jesus being about six weeks old when this took place and, therefore, didn't take up space explaining this concept. We need it explained to us.

While you still have your Bible opened to Luke, turn to chapter five. Read the first eleven verses. Have you ever been fishing? Did you do it at night? I'm guessing, that unless you were doing some sort of illegal jug fishing somewhere you probably did the fishing during the daylight hours. It might have been an ungodly early hour of the morning, but day nonetheless. So, Jesus tells Peter to go back out and fish, even though Peter and his kid brother were done and putting up the nets. Peter says they fished all night long. You might be thinking, "Well, the fish were all asleep, so get back out there and catch something!"

The Bible Survival Manual:

In fact, the fish are asleep, so to speak, at night. They also come up into the shallower parts of the Galilean sea to spend the night. Fishing was, therefore, done at night with nets. Jesus (the carpenter) was telling Peter (the professional fisherman) to break two rules of fishing in that area of the world: go out during the day and go out into the deep water! But concentrating on this information, we will note that this isn't explained in the Bible. Those in the first century, especially those from the Galilean area who were fishermen, would know a little about fishing and know that Jesus went against the norm. In short, a miracle occurred.

In a modern day correlation, each reader probably has a pretty good idea of what a fireman does. You may have never been a fireman, or even be related to one, but you have a pretty good idea. That's what I mean by Theophilus having a pretty good idea about the Jewish baby laws and a small grasp of Galilean fishing. He might have even possessed a small idea about synagogue worship as we shall see in the next example.

Without leaving Luke, take the time to read in chapter four starting with verse 14. When you get to verse 16 we are told that Jesus stood up to read, and a scroll from Isaiah the prophet was handed to him. Stood up to read! So, you say, "So what? My Preacher stands up every week to preach." Again, unplug from 21st century America and plug into first century Palestine, especially the Jewish synagogue. Quite a bit is in those four words, enough to set those folks in the synagogue on their ears! I'll leave that one to you to chase down, but when you do chase it down, you will see what all was involved in those four words: *stood up to read*. In fact, I gave this particular verse a week's space on my weekly website.

That wasn't a shameless bit of self-promotion [Are you *sure?!*], just telling you where you can go to chase that one down. Well, OK, maybe a tiny bit of self-promotion, but it fascinates me every time I read that passage, even after all these years. One last illustration, then we will get on with it. For many, many years I have seen folks sit around in an adult Sunday school, discussing John 9:6. Some are sort of 'grossed out,' while others offer explanations about certain sons' spittle believed to contain magical powers. Yes, there was a belief about that, but only for the seventh son--not the firstborn. And

## Mystifying to Manageable

the seventh son phenomenon was more of a Hellenistic/pagan belief, not Jewish. I'm not sure that Joseph and Mary had that many sons, but it doesn't matter for Jesus was the firstborn anyway. Jesus spit on the ground in defiance of a made-up Jewish law concerning spitting on the ground being defined as work since the end product was clay or mud--and so He did it on the Sabbath—and John tells us so! Cool, huh?!

Preparation in the way of reading of times and customs can go a long way in helping knock out some of the questions that will arise when reading through the Bible. But what about commentaries? Why haven't I given any space to them in this section of preparing one for studying the Bible except to infer that they somehow carry the number '666' with them?

Don't get me wrong about commentaries. They CAN be helpful. They can have a wealth of information in them, including times and customs that we've been discussing up to now. Even written one myself on the little letter of Jude which is both highly interpretive and highly applicable--and I'm told it falls into the helpful category. But they can be damaging, especially when they become the front line in trying to unlock the Bible.

Go back and look at the name again: commentary. It is a person's thoughts and conclusions (comments) about what is written in the Bible. We, as writers, may have come to the right conclusions, or we may not have! If your introduction to a certain book of the Bible or section of Scripture is a wrong commentary then you will, because of human nature, have the same wrong conclusion as the author of that commentary and all of this before you get out of the chute. This is why I would hand folks a Bible instead of a commentary when they came lurking around my office looking for a study help so they could teach a book of the Bible on the following Sunday.

If you don't believe me about commentaries, then try this little exercise. You may have to go bug your Pastor or hit the church library to do so. Grab a commentary written in the sixties. Not the 1960's, but the 1860's. [Didn't he just tell us to *not* get a commentary from the minister?!] Then grab one from the Depression/WWII era. Finally, grab one written in the last decade. If you speak a second language, then pick up one of those also regardless of when it was written. Find some topic or passage that you or someone else considers hard or controversial. Compare what folks were thinking 150 years ago to what they think today--and all points in-between including other cultures! You will find that things change. Sometimes vastly so. It is impossible for a writer to divorce himself from his 'life and times.' You may wonder if I have a specific topic in mind. I do. Try the one on women being silent in the church found in First Corinthians chapter 14. That ought to keep you busy for a month or so--and vastly entertained--but it will forever prove my point and be burned into your brain.

And in another closely related vein, this is why I would give people the same answer that Jesus gave his questioner in Luke 10:26 (when He counter-asked, "What is written in the Law? How does it read to you?") if they came up and asked me a question such as, "Preach, what do we believe about such and such...?" I know what *I* believe, but I didn't (can't) know what that person believes. I may *think* I know what they *need* to believe (because it is my job), but that's not my call. As much as I might want to (gasp!) pass on to them the Party Line, it is to their detriment if I do. We've got to become, first and foremost, a people of the Book.

When you become a 'people of the Book' you will cease to be a Nod. A Nod is someone who can only nod their head when something is said from the pulpit or in front of the Sunday morning Bible class, especially, and simply, because the person is a dynamic speaker wearing a power tie.

One of the most dynamic speakers I will ever know once gave a bunch of us Preacher Boys a lesson on this very concept in the obligatory chapel that started each day in Bible Boot Camp. He was preaching along, waving his hands and raising his voice. He made a quick point or two--followed by raising his hands and his Bible in the air--and a cascade of sharp 'Amens!' came forth from the audience as folks were caught up in the emotional intensity of the lesson.

He stopped dead mid-sentence and said, "You weren't listening to me. Don't 'amen' that...don't 'amen' that. It is wrong!" As best as I can remember, there was an extra paper to write that week and a bit more time in the school library, but a lesson well learned: don't be a Nod. Be a person of the Book.

# Propprecids

I thought this was quite clever, and you will undoubtedly agree. **Propprecids** stands for **Pre**judice, **Op**inions and **Pre**conceived **Id**eas (See? It was clever!). So, what is so terrible about having prejudice, opinions or preconceived ideas? OK, let's break down each of these three words and examine them, beginning with the word prejudice.

In today's lingo, prejudice is tied up with the word race, meaning skin color. We know this is bad, and wish it would go away. We also know the damage that it can do when it is passed onto our children, then our children's children. Children get shunned. Children get hurt. Children get dead. It's a bad, bad word. Sadly, some folks don't even try to curb their prejudice towards their fellow man, but what about prejudice in the religious arena?

We do have folks that hang about the various church buildings Sunday after Sunday that are still all caught up in the hatred which is attached to the various colors of skin that we are all packaged in, however, as horrible and demeaning as that might be, I'm going a different direction with the word prejudice so we can include a larger arena.

Before we go any further, we need to revisit one of those two-dollar words we've already seen. The word is *isogesis*. Yep, it's that two dollar word we read earlier and one that needs to be avoided at all cost. Exegesis is what we are looking for when we do Bible study. Without going into the great word study that I'm just chomping at the horse to do, lemme give you the simple meaning: *Isogesis* is placing meaning *into* the text and *exegesis* is gathering meaning *from* the text. The former is bad, the latter is good.

Let's put it another way. How many times have you said, or heard someone say, "They are just making the Bible say

The Bible Survival Manual:

what they want it to say..."? That is the endpoint of isogesis. When you break down *prejudice* you get *pre-judged*. Someone has predetermined what the verse or chapter or section is to say. They have proof texted (hey, remember that discussion?) and are only going to the particular passage to back up what they want to say. Be thinking along the lines of prejudice the next time you hear some absurd thing and you're thinking, "Hey, they took that out of context!" They probably did, and probably did so on purpose--to shore up some long held belief.

Opinions and preconceived ideas aren't far behind prejudice, although usually they aren't as malicious as the prejudice. But, sadly, we need to take the time to see just where these opinions and preconceived ideas originate from. In a word: one's past.

OK, that was two words, but that's not important right now and let's keep moving. You grew up attending a Sunday school, let's say, and you have formed an opinion about God, His Son, the Bible, Sunday happenings between ten thirty and noon, what the man on center stage is called and what he (and you!) should wear, the works. Then one day you decide to come out of your childhood and begin to read this Book for yourself. You will come to the Bible--the very first time you attempt to read it--with all of the part and parcel of your background. The problem is, this background may be right dead on or it may be totally wrong or probably something in-between!

I'm searching for an opinion or preconception to use as an illustration. The only problem being is that there are literally *thousands* that can stump or otherwise thwart a good study of the Scriptures. Let's take one from the turn of last century in this country as an example. It has to do with wine. I can already hear jaw hinges squeaking as gravity takes hold of the lower half.

Now, before we get into the illustration of drinking fermented or distilled beverages, did something jump up in the back of your mind? Did an emotion stir in there, somewhere? Did a face from your ever present past jump up before you-- good or bad? For the majority of folks reading this book, I'm willing to bet that each of these questions will illicit some sort of response. If so, then mission accomplished! Read on...

For instance, let's say that a person is just convinced that the drinking of any type of fermented or distilled beverage is forbidden in the Bible. Some folks in this country were convinced of the same thing over a hundred years ago. They would pull Bible verses out here and there to 'prove' that they were right about God not wanting any type of fermentation to pass human lips. Time rocked on, bars were literally hatcheted to splinters and an amendment was passed to the Constitution of the United States that forbade any type of alcohol altogether. Well, we all know where that led.

Organized crime sprang up. Thousands of jobs went by the wayside. Thousands of illegal jobs sprang forth. Folks got hurt. Folks got dead. A repeal followed after a long dozen years but the type of crime the Great Noble Experiment produced has never left us. Furthermore, we can trace a large chunk of the ganglands of today right back to the gangs of the Roaring 20's and Depression 30's. You think it's a leap to go from a misapplied Bible concept, complete with the hype, to gangs in our cities and towns today? Do some sociological study yourself and see if the thread isn't there. The case has been made by better folks than I. But enough of the history lesson and back on preconceptions and opinions. Just remember what we are to do with history lessons.

["Did he just say that the church is partly responsible for those gangs we have in our town that we keep trying to shy our children away from?" "Y'now, I think he did?" "Well, I'll declare!"]

The opinions held by the teetotalers were stronger than their desire to look at Scripture and come away with a right view which included such items as moderation and a healthy dose of Romans 14:1-15:7. Sure, I'll be the first to admit that alcohol in its many forms has done way too much damage in some folk's lives. That is because of excessive use and misuse. That is always bad on any subject such as gambling and even eating out at fast food joints or continuously plopping down in front of the television for hours on end. But when the teetotalers looked at places in the Bible where Jesus turned water into wine, or ate and drank with 'sinners and tax collectors,' they cannot see the beauty of the miracle or the love Jesus had for the common man for fussing, humphing and musing about

The Bible Survival Manual:

how that must have been unfermented grape juice and on and on (and on!) and they missed the lesson altogether.

To these folks, some of which survive today, it would seem that a forbiddance of alcohol is about the only thing that the Bible is concerned with. You don't become one of those folks. You study.

Dipping back into prejudice--the kind we usually think about--I had an encounter with a man one Saturday summer afternoon that I hope I never have again. The church family I was ministering to on the east coast was just about split 50/50 white and black. Toss in one Korean lady for good measure. One of our elders in the church family was black. Come to think of it, he probably still is. We were having one of those 'come spruce up the church building' Saturdays. I was close to the circle drive checking the mailbox and the aforementioned elder was off in the south forty on the riding mower whacking weeds with a forty-two inch swath. An older white man drove up and begin to engage me with talk. Seems he was looking for a place to attend the next day to 'worship God in spirit and in truth.' Check my reasonable facsimile on the back cover to see what flavor God made me.

The gentleman asked me if this was, indeed, the true church. I told him that, yes, we are a God believing, Bible following bunch of redeemed folks. He asked me if only true Christians worshipped here. I began to sniff a rodent and said, "Yes, we have many good and honest Christians here." He then pointed off in the distance to my elder and said, "Well, what then is that?" I smelt more than a rodent at that point and said, "That brother is one of the finest disciples of Jesus I know. He's one of our Shepherds here."

The conversation deteriorated extremely fast from that point forward. I did ask him just what verse in the Bible or passage or *anything* in-between the covers of the Bible would give him the right to believe that only white folks could be saved. He went to John 4:35 and quoted, "Look on the fields that they are *white* for harvest."

Prejudice, preconceived notion and opinion all rolled into one! I'm sure that if he is still alive today he would have something to say about the 'White House' in Washington, DC. Now, the next question you are wanting to ask is, "Did you

Mystifying to Manageable

hit him?" OK, now you've asked it and let's move on. But you can certainly see where opinions and such can hamper any attempt to sit down and really try to read the Scriptures and gain any meaning out of them.

Another item that preconceived notions and conclusions will hamper is the ability to sit down and read ALL of the Bible. When one is stuck on a certain thought or notion, it is self limiting. Like scum rising to the top of a stagnant pond, your preconception will loom large in your mind like the bar smashing, hatcheting teetotalers of a century gone by. As stated before, one would think in talking with them that alcohol prohibition was all there was in the Bible. Talk with Old Broken Nose and you would think that Whitey Righty goes to Heaven was the only subject in the Bible. Prejudiced, opinionated and folks full of preconceptions are like that: they can quickly reduce the Bible to one or two little pet peeve subjects and then irritate everyone around them.

And so, here's a good place to talk about eschatology which is a fancy term for the end of the world or the end of times. Sort of high on the list in today's religious thought. To talk with some, you would think that the only subject in the Bible was the end of times. Nothing could be farther from the truth (Farther, or further? Let me know). In fact, most of the Bible is taken up with man needing to learn how to imitate God and His ways and treat your fellow neighbor like you would want to be treated! Little is actually written about the end of time. Read the entire Bible and see if I'm not right.

So, how does one identify his opinions and preconceptions and check them at the door when it comes to reading the Bible? I'm not one-hundred percent sure on that one. I do have a couple of tricks up my sleeve in helping to identify areas that can be preconceptions or opinions or even prejudices (as ugly as they are). First, listen to your group. What group? Whatever group you hang with under the banner of religion.

Is your Bible discussion group stuck on one thing or another? Does your Pastor sound like a broken record in one area of the Bible? Is your Preacher constantly hammering one point home at the expense of the thousands of points that could be covered every week? A broken record is a tell-tale for

The Bible Survival Manual:

preconceptions. After you've listened to your group, listen to yourself.

Are *you* hung up on one thing or another? Does every Bible discussion come back around to the same old idea time and time again? Here's a hard hitting one: does your small group cringe when your hand goes up wanting to be called upon to speak? You, yourself, might be hung up and high centered on an opinion or a prejudice somewhere. It is true, there's more to the Bible than _____--and you will need to fill in the blank!

If you need a down to earth example of what was in the last few paragraphs, then I would ask you to log onto the Westboro Baptist Church website and see what I mean by high centering on one aspect of their 'understanding' of the Bible. Yes, these are the koo-koo nuts in Topeka, Kansas who run around picketing funerals, rallies, seminars, church services and everything with those 'God Hates Fags' signs. My advice is to not look at their website on a full stomach. Same rules as swimming apply: wait thirty minutes before you surf Westboro's website after a meal.

Now, for sure they are extreme, but they are an extreme example of a one-tracked mind. They cannot see *anything* in the Bible but homosexuality, so *everything*, including the love of God, get's turned back to that topic. Actually, I've not seen anything on their website about the love of God so I may have to revise that in later editions, but you get my point.

These three no-no's: prejudice, preconceptions and opinions (Just say 'NO' to PPO's!), will seriously hamper or even kill your endeavor to read the Bible. It may be a close friend or relative that points them out to you by saying, "You're always talking about such and such. Don't you ever think of anything else?" That might be another clue that you have fallen in the no-no trap. Want another example, benign as it is? I love to drag this one out once a year.

Every Christmas, there are manger scenes with Mary, Joseph and the baby Jesus all closely crowded by animals, shepherds and...three wise men. This is borne out either in plastic figurines in yards or on stage at many a local church building. Cute kids with strapped on beards. But is there any scriptural basis for this gathering?

Mystifying to Manageable

Matthew chapter 3 starts with the words *Now after Jesus was born in Bethlehem of Judea...*, the keyword here being 'after.' How much after? Well, we know by further reading that the magi arrived at the house that the family had moved to. Later, when Herod found he had been tricked by the Magi, or wise men, he had all the babies from two year old and down slaughtered. Why two years old if Jesus had just been born the night before? Now is where you throw in your ciphering powers and figure it out. Be sure and toss into your ciphering bag the fact that the magi were *following* the star that appeared the night that Jesus was born in Bethlehem. How long did they follow it?

And another thing, who said anything about three Magi? They presented *gifts* that were made up of three types of items, but that's the only 'three' you will find there. There could have just as easily have been two magi, or even seven. Perhaps there were five and they pooled their resources and bought three kinds of gifts. So what?

The last two paragraphs are widely known, however, the point is this: we are unwilling to budge *one inch* at Christmas time due to our traditions, plus the fact that we would have a surplus of plastic bearded wise men in sets of three collecting dust. Also, what would we do with the three bearded children, put them in the circus?

With that on your mind, I wanted you to see just how easy it is for tradition (which is formed in part by **Propprecids**) to slide into--and remain permanently--in our 'understanding' of the Bible. We, the church, put on Christmas plays, in part, for the unbelievers to be moved. They go home, pick up a Bible and read about what they just saw. They come to the conclusion that we don't have a clue what we're talking about because we messed up the story...

Is there some sort of evil lurking in the fact that we crowd magi in with donkeys and shepherds? Will the fact that we, once again, prop up the plastic wise men or strap beards on the next little generation to play the magi keep otherwise good, honest and well intending disciples of Christ out of Heaven? No, let's reiterate one more time. This is simply a well known illustration to show how tradition, among other things, can play a heavy hand in our 'understanding' of the

The Bible Survival Manual:

Scriptures. It slides in, much like those folks Jude was talking about in Jude verse four: crept in unnoticed. Worth taking the time to both ponder this illustration and remain on the lookout for other items!

Come to the Scriptures with an open mind. You are coming to be taught. You are not coming to shore up something you've always wanted to be true or *thought* was true. You are not coming to the Bible to prove your next door neighbor, or pew buddy on Sunday, wrong on this or that doctrinal point. You are coming to the Bible to be taught by God--molded into what He wants you to know and be--as a disciple of His.

Finally, as we close this section let's go back and review Mr. Naaman again. Remember, he said, "I thought," but he <u>thought wrong</u>. He was prejudiced, opinionated and full of preconceived ideas. If we are like him, we will be wrong--just as he was, even if nothing more than our attitudes. We really do create that box over time. Stay well away from sliding into that coffin.

Remember, by themselves, such items as bearded children may not amount to anything by themselves. It is when these small items grow and multiply that understanding gets out of hand. It might be time well spent to make a list of items or subjects or words that you are high centered on when you spend your time in the Scriptures. Maybe a little sticky note in the back cover of your Bible. Be honest with yourself. God was honest when He had the Bible written down over all those centuries, so we should respond in like kind.

The longer I live in this world, being well over a half century at this point, the more I have come to understand that honesty, in and of itself, is not something that comes naturally to us human beans. I'm beginning to believe that it is something that we must reach and strive for on a continual, uninterrupted, basis. Honesty is one of the main ingredients of repentance. It also plays a huge part in the carrying out of the first two verses of Romans chapter twelve. Actually, it is interwoven in our spiritual maturity, if not our entire walk with God while on Planet Here. Let's stop before I start another book. Just be honest with yourself and God. It will pay off.

# Reading the Bible

So you are ready to get into your Bible. You have turned off the television, put your cellphone on standby and locked all children in the attic. [He's not being nice!] Actually on further thought, just lock your specific children up and not the neighbor's children. People will talk and you will be labeled. But anyway, your distractions are now gone. You have flushed your mind of all preconceived notions and opinions and you want to look at the Bible fresh. The only question remains as to where in the Bible to start? Perhaps treat it like any other book and begin with page one...

One could start with Genesis and read straight through to Revelation. Many have done that and will continue to do so till God puts a stop to all of this. You start with Genesis and read *In the beginning*... and you would be correct: you would be at the beginning. Genesis has a lot of firsts. First folks, first languages, first nations, first promise of salvation, first judgment of God, first covenant, and the list goes on till you end Genesis and find Jacob's family secure in Egypt during the God-directed famine.

Then comes Exodus. Now *that's* a thrilling book. Slavery, plagues, snakes swallowing up other snakes, frogs everywhere, folks running around all worried, the exodus from Egypt through a path in the water, gathering at Mount Sinai for the Big Ten, wandering through the desert drinking water from a rock, eating quail from the sky and gathering manna from wherever manna came from. One cannot put the book of Exodus down for wanting to see what happens next. Then comes the end of Exodus and you turn to the next book: Leviticus. You begin reading: "Then the Lord called to Moses and spoke to him from the tent of meeting, saying...," and a list of rules coupled with various sacrifices begins to come cascading down.

The Bible Survival Manual:

Leviticus is true. Leviticus is part of the Bible. Leviticus is the 'fleshing out' of the Big Ten so to speak. And let's face it, Leviticus is, well, if you are new to the Bible or new to really sitting down and getting all you can get from the Bible so you can be all you can be, then Leviticus can be an exercise in trying to figure out just what in the world is going on. Leviticus seems to be rooted in the 3-R's: repetition, repetition, repetition!

The Bible is one book that you are excused from reading from the front to the back. Why? Because it is, in reality, sixty six different entries that all point in their own way to one central figure and that is Jesus, the Christ. The four gospel accounts (the first four books of the New Testament) tell the story of Jesus while He was here on earth among men. The fifth book of the New Testament, Acts of the Apostles, gives us the happenings just after Jesus left for Heaven and turned the growing of the church over to the apostles.

The rest of the New Testament is various writings showing what happened (or should be happening!) after His church was established. That leaves us with the Old Testament. What's up with the Old Testament?

In a word: shadow. When you see a shadow as you approach a corner in downtown Anywhere, USA, you can pretty much tell whether what is about to come around the corner is a dog, a child or a motorcycle. That's what shadows do. They aren't the reality, but they let you know what the reality is going to be. And that, in a nutshell, is our Old Testament. All of the Garden of Eden, Noah floating around with a boat load of animals, the exodus from Egypt through the Red Sea, wandering in the wilderness, resting on the Sabbath day, crossing Jordan and entering the Promised Land are all shadows--and the reality is Christ.

And what about those sacrifices? All of the bulls and goats and turtle doves for this offering or that offering was nothing more than a foreshadowing of Jesus Christ and His ultimate sacrifice on the cross. How do I know this? Well, I've just spoiled the book of Hebrews for you, but I've written all of this in order to drive a point home: it's best if you find a different way to read the Bible other than cover to cover. And if you have no idea what I'm talking about, or are confused as to what all this shadow/reality talk means, then bear with me

Mystifying to Manageable

and read on. It will, hopefully, come to light a bit farther down in the discussion. [I'll just bet he will have a suggestion long about here...]

I have a suggestion...which I will toss in for free, just for purchasing this book: approach the Bible with the different types of writings in mind. Here is what I have come up with. Others have their lists, here is mine. Many would prefer *The Divisions of the Bible* instead. However, with some complications (chronological order at the forefront), I strongly believe that <u>styles</u> and <u>classifications</u> should be dealt with.

Consider the following, and remember what we discussed about the Old Testament being a huge shadow for the reality of Jesus, the Christ. I will have some notes as to why I classified some entries as I did. I think it is best to save the notes till the end so the continuity won't be broken up too much. Here it is:

- **History of the Forming of the Jewish Nation**: Genesis; Exodus; Leviticus; Numbers; Deuteronomy
- **History of the Jewish Nation in Canaan (Promised) Land**: Joshua; Judges; Ruth; I&II Samuel; I&II Kings; I&II Chronicles; Ezra; Nehemiah; Esther
- **Wisdom Literature**: Job; Psalms; Proverbs; Ecclesiastics; Song of Solomon; Revelation
- **Writings of the Prophets**: Isaiah; Jeremiah; Lamentations; Ezekiel; Daniel; Hosea; Joel; Amos; Obadiah; Jonah; Mica; Nahum; Habakkuk; Zephaniah; Haggai; Zechariah; Malachi
- **Biography of Jesus' Life & Ministry**: Matthew; Mark; Luke; John; Acts
- **Congregational or At-large Letters**: Acts chapter 15; Romans; I&II Corinthians; Galatians; Ephesians; Philippians; Colossians; I&II Thessalonians; Hebrews; James; I&II Peter; I&II John; Jude; Revelation chapters 2 & 3
- **Individual Letters**: I&II Timothy; Titus; Philemon; III John; Luke; Acts

I put Esther in with the history of the Jews in Canaan. I know that they were not in Canaan during this particular story but they were *supposed* to be there! A little thing called Babylonian captivity got in their way. Even when they were allowed to go back to Jerusalem and rebuild the temple, some stayed behind.

I've also included Revelation into the Wisdom literature, since it was written to give wisdom to the early church during the time of persecution. I like this better than Apocalypse (as in 'uncover' or 'reveal'). The entire Bible *could* be, *would* be and is in need of uncovering if we don't understand what is being said or put brain grease into the understanding thereof. More, much more, on brain grease later in this book.

Then, there is the need for the placing of the books of Luke and Acts into Jesus' Life and Ministry. You will note that both books were listed twice (along with some other entries and partials such as chapters). And for Acts, this isn't just because Jesus takes center stage in chapter one, but because of the first few words of this second letter that Luke wrote to Theophilus. It is an account of all that Jesus *began* to do, but was finished by His Apostles, mainly Peter, John and then Paul.

Oops!! What about the so-called *missing books of the Bible?!* Gopher-it! In reality, there is nothing whatsoever along the lines of soteriology in these books. By soteriology, I mean salvation issues. They are writings. They are writings from antiquity, however, they do not contain any prophecies that point to the Christ, which is the central theme of the entire Bible. (um, and neither is there in Ruth, Kings, Esther, Ezra...... but for another time). If you would like to read these 'lost' books, they are usually included in Bibles that are printed under the eye of the Catholic church, or they can be bought separately in any religious bookstore.

If I were you, just for fun, I'd buy them from a bookstore and make the clerk's day. You will say, "I'm looking for the lost books of the Bible." The clerk will say, as he hands you a copy of the Apocrypha, "Here, I just found them. Not lost anymore!" I'm guessing that book clerks get a big kick out of stuff like this. Back on track...

Since the central theme of the Bible points toward--and is wrapped up in--Jesus Christ, I highly recommend that the serious student of the Bible start with the New Testament, especially the Gospel accounts. And they should be read in this order: Mark, John, Matthew, First Luke and then followed lastly with Second Luke. Yes, I'm being a smarty pants on the last two entries, but look at the opening verses of Luke and compare with the opening verses of Acts. It may come as a surprise to you that these two entries were personal letters to the same individual. A little more background and I will give you the rationale behind the starting lineup for your reading endeavor.

Most of the New Testament is composed of letters, not really books as we count books. Even First and Second Luke are, in reality, letters (*cf* Lk 1:1-4/Acts 1:1). Out of the twenty-seven entries in the New Testament, twenty-three are outright letters. In the book of Revelation there are seven letters embedded in chapters 2 & 3. The letter in Acts chapter 15 is nearly as long as the letter we call Second John!

The first five books of the New Testament contain the story of Jesus, followed by the spreading of the church (in Acts). That, in a nutshell, is what Jesus came to this earth, as one of us, to accomplish: build His church. Take the time to read Matthew chapter 16. The rest of the New Testament, though not nearly in chronological order, is the various writers (some apostles, some not) giving instructions, solving problems and generally tweaking the church to be all that she could be. Some churches shone brightly, others did not. Same is true today and will be tomorrow.

Just like jumping into an infomercial during the conclusion, little is gained by jumping into a letter such as Colossians or James or (gasp!) Revelation and trying to make sense out of the church--with all her problems and shortcomings--if the basic teachings of Jesus, inclusive of His life, are not read first and understood. Now back to the order of reading the beginning of the New Testament.

I don't really believe that the student of the Bible needs to understand all of the finer points of the Law of Moses that the Jews of Jesus' day were (supposed) to be living by just to read and understand the story of Jesus. If you would like to review the Big Ten, they can be found in Exodus chapter 20 and again in Deuteronomy chapter 5. Just know that, not unlike today's scene, the religious leaders of Jesus' day had tacked on quite a number of man made rules on top of the Ten Commandments. They had elevated themselves to the place of rule maker, gatekeeper and judge, making it very, very difficult for the common worshipper of God.

I don't know about you, but that last paragraph is ringing ever so true in this day and age, also! Funny how that works out.

So, why start with Mark? Because it is the shortest of the five books I've mentioned? In one sense, yes, but in another sense it is the way that Mark is written. It is a book that is more concerned with what Jesus *did* rather than what he *said*. You have, perhaps, heard the old adage about seeing a sermon rather than hearing one? Well, that is Mark, so you will get extra points if you start with the Gospel of Mark [just *who* is passing points out?].

One word that stands out in Mark is the word 'immediately'(in the New American Standard Bible) or some word like it (such as, "at that very time...") which conveys the same meaning. You will find it dozens of times. One will get the sense that Jesus was a busy, busy teacher when reading Mark. Yes, there are parables and other teachings, but the focus in Mark is what Jesus did, who He did it with or to, where He was at when He did these things, and the consequences of His actions. Mark doesn't even concern himself with the birth of the Christ, rather he opens with John the Baptizer already at work and within a few verses in comes Jesus, is baptized by John in less than a dozen verses, and is off and running with His ministry.

The key phrase in Mark is found in the opening sentence: "This is the beginning of the Good News about Jesus Christ, the Son of God." Everything in Mark's writing past that opening verse is the story of the Good News, which is what the word *gospel* means!

Then, after reading Mark, one would do best by reading the Gospel of John. You may have heard John being called the non-synoptic gospel. Fancy, fancy, but this just means that John didn't write his account of Jesus in the same way--or from the same vantage point--that Matthew, Mark and Luke wrote. John has a different viewpoint, probably writing his account many years after the other three. John didn't want to just produce another narrative of the life and times of Jesus, the Christ.

John's viewpoint is not so much what Jesus *did* as it is what He *said*. Indeed, if you were to take a weekend or some great block of time and try to put the actual days together that John shows us, you would come up with far less than two weeks out of the life of Jesus. Some, including myself, find only about a collective week out of the life of Jesus. If you have one of those red letter Bibles (where the words of Jesus are printed with red ink), then scan down the book of John and see just how much of it is in red. Quite fascinating, don't you think?

Sometimes in John, chapter after chapter is taken up with what Jesus said, whether it was teaching the masses, trying to teach the Pharisees, or simply talking with the Father through the avenue of prayer. Mark gives you an account of how Jesus lived and interacted with us. John gives you an account of why Jesus lived the way He did.

Is there a key phrase in John like we saw in Mark? Yes there is, but it isn't at the beginning of the writing but close to the end. Most scholars would say that John's statement in 20:30 would be the main statement of the book. I can't think of a better one than this, unless it is John 1:50: "you will see greater things than these!"

Now you have finished John. You have finished two different accounts of the life and ministry of Jesus, the focal point of the entire Bible. You also have the great urge to now jump off into Galatians, or First Corinthians or (yikes!) Revelation--or go back and tackle Leviticus.

Resist the urge! Go join Read-ahead Anonymous. Staple shut Romans 1:1 through concordance. Do *something* to keep yourself on track. I can all but guarantee you that you will appreciate the Bible much, much more if you know all there is to know about Jesus, the Christ, before you tackle King Jehoshaphat, Balaam's talking donkey, the Tower of Babel or anything else in the pages of the Bible. Next stop in the New Testament: Matthew. [Betcha he's got a reason for making it third!]

Here's the reason I'm making Matthew third on the list: the Jews were looking for a Messiah when Jesus came here among us. Yes, some of them knew their Old Testament prophecies well. Scribes and lawyers were searching the Scriptures looking for the Anointed One to come. They (sort of) had the right idea of the Messiah, however, they were looking for a type of earthly king to once again sit on the throne of David

The Bible Survival Manual:

in downtown Jerusalem--and as an added bonus, boot the Roman occupational army back to the Italian boot. In comes Matthew's account.

There is a genealogy at the beginning of Matthew. It won't be the last one you will run across in the New Testament (or the Bible for that matter). It is quite all right if you stumble and bumble your way through the names. It's even allowed to sort of skip on down towards the end of the list of names. Just remember that the list is there at the beginning of Matthew, and it is there for a reason!

Then later, when you are hip deep into Old Testament history about the kings of Judah (which, surprisingly can be found in First and Second Kings along with the kings of Israel--how about that), you can come back to this list at the beginning of Matthew and find the kings of Judah in a direct line from David to Jesus. You'll find a few kings left out of the list along with some minor name spelling changes. Sort of like 'Kathy' and 'Cathy' but no biggie diffs. A king is a king. This gives us some insight into the 'why' of Matthew's writing.

Matthew wanted to show that Jesus is, indeed, *The King* that everyone was looking for. He might have had a somewhat humble beginning, had no real place to call home while He taught and ministered, and even had to borrow a tomb for a few days since He was not a property owner (nor was He necessarily needing the tomb long term), but He was *The King* nonetheless. Jesus, according to Matthew, was here both *on* a mission and *for* a mission. That mission was to show Himself as *The King*.

This is why Matthew spends time on the bearded Magi, or Wise Men coming to honor Jesus as King. Matthew also spends time on King Herod both pouting about his kingship *not* being honored and subsequent eradication of the male children in Bethlehem and surrounding villages. John and Mark spend no time on Jesus' birth. Luke? We'll get to him, hold your britches.

Matthew also spends time on the showdown between Satan and Jesus in chapter four. John and Mark spend no time on Jesus' temptation. Luke? We'll get to him, hold your britches.

Kings have to have a kingdom or they really aren't a king at all. One cannot be the King of Outer Bogwana if there is

Mystifying to Manageable

no such place. You have to have subjects, too, in order to be a king. If Outer Bogwana is uninhabited with folks, or just full of penguins and rhinos, then the king is the king of lots of empty space, penguins, rhinos--and not a king at all. Kings rule a place full of subjects. This brings us to the main verse, or theme, of the Book of Matthew.

This isn't found at the beginning like Mark, nor even at the end like John. This theme is found smack dab in the middle of the book. Try the little discussion Jesus has with his followers about His church in Matthew chapter 16. There you have it: a place with subjects. The place is the whole world and the subjects of the kingdom are folks like you and me. Time may pass and folks like you and me are no longer here, but we're still in the kingdom under The King.

Yep, as time marches on the Kingdom of Heaven just gets bigger and bigger. Drives Satan batty.

Now, it is time for Luke, parts one and two. I'm not trying to beat a dead horse here. Actually, that may be riding a dead horse and beating a dead cat. Either way, I can't stress enough that Luke wrote twice to a fella named Theophilus. We have chosen to call the first letter The *Gospel According to Luke* and the second letter *The Book of the Acts of the Apostles*. Why? I haven't a clue!

Then, we go off to seminaries, lectureships and pulpits and start throwing out all this stuff about the gospel here and the book of Acts there and start fights and divide folks and claim that there isn't anything in Acts except history then someone comes along and says there is soteriology in there. One group states that Luke is inspired and Acts is not and another group yells, "For crying out loud what are they talking about?" Then the music stops and everyone tries to grab a chair and then the music starts over again and everyone starts going once again in a circle...

Oh, for Pete's sake! They are *two* letters written by the *same* man to the *same* recipient and they are both full of *very good stuff!* There are two very good reasons that I chose Luke as the last writer. The first has to do with our occidental mind if you live here in the western hemisphere like I do, or perhaps in

The Bible Survival Manual:

western Europe or off upside down in Australia (do they know they're standing with their heads pointing down? I wonder...).

We like stories that start at the beginning and move toward a conclusion. I don't know about you, but it takes a very good author or film maker to hold my attention if he (yes, or she) keeps bouncing back and forth from the past to the future and hardly slowing down in the here and now! I get confused and have to go get popcorn.

I'm not advocating that you go back and reread Mark, John and Matthew, but you may have noticed that Jesus may be in one place, then suddenly be in another! While it is true He could do that if He wanted to (and did after His resurrection), He didn't do that as a regular course of action. The answer lies in the fact that it is a Jewish way of writing. The next two paragraphs are vitally important and should be remembered till the end of time:

We, here in the western part of the world, like chronological order. Writers in that part of the world grouped stuff in general in a different way. Take Matthew chapter 13 for instance. All those parables all scrunched up together. Really? No, that's the way Matthew (very much an oriental Jew) grouped them. Mark (a half Jew on Mama's side) had some similar groupings long about chapter 5. Mark only half thought like you and I think. Lots of healing and casting out demons and such. That's just the way they got grouped.

Let's put this another way for illustration. An oriental mind is writing along and decides to now write about six. We ask, "Six what?" because we like order, order, order. The oriental mind continues with six: six days, six people, six parables, six in the evening, six concepts then six lepers. Then, they move on to red: Red Sea, red sunsets, red banners, red-faced church leaders and finally red cars.

Luke, however, wasn't a Jew. He was Greek. He thought like you and I think. Look carefully at the opening verses of Luke's Gospel account (First Luke). Notice that he's telling Theophilus (a fellow occidental...you can tell by the Latin name) that he is getting ready to write out things <u>in consecutive order</u> after <u>lots of careful inquiry</u>. You go, Luke!

And let the first few verses of Luke's Gospel stand for both the prime mover and the focal point of what he ends up writing. But is this going to stand for the book of Acts, also? In a sense, yes, he is merely sending part two to his friend or acquaintance. However, look carefully at the opening lines of the Book of Acts.

Here, Luke is telling Theophilus (and us, *that's* why he's called Theophil-us! OK, not really) that he is going beyond Jesus' ministry while here on earth. Jesus began to do and teach some things and now has left it in the hands of His followers. Luke wants to tell that story, also. Jesus came to set up His church and one of the things he set up was that His followers would kick it into high gear. Take a few minutes and compare Jesus' prayer to the Father found in John chapter 17 with what Luke wrote at the beginning of Acts of the Apostles. How quickly it all comes together.

Well, you've read the story of Jesus (four times now) and the early church. By the end of Acts the church is rocking and rolling along. Any problems? Are you kidding me? They had as many problems then as we do now. In fact, it seems to be the *same* problems today as they had back then. So, it would seem that if the church today would just sit down and read their Bibles... So we now come to what to read next.

Now, it is time to read the letters. There are many to choose from. Go back and look at the dividing up of the Bible and see that there are personal letters, letters to certain cities meaning certain churches, and open letters intended to be read first here and then sent there. Any suggestions? Of course!

Try Ephesians...or at least that is what we have come to call that particular letter. In the most reliable (notice I didn't say the oldest) Greek manuscripts the words *at Ephesus* in the opening lines cannot be supported. Best guess is that it was one of those circular letters intended first here, then there, then the next place, but probably landed finally in the city of Ephesus and the name stuck. It will always be called Ephesians so just might as well get used to it. But it is a unique book.

Great chapter divisions, for once, especially in the middle! Yep, the book with the worst verse breaks has the best chapter breaks. Well, there you go! Chapters one, two and three concern themselves with some facts about God and His church. Chapters four, five and six concern themselves with

The Bible Survival Manual:

the *so what*. If I were you I would try to get used to those two words *so what* and keep them handy. Pull them out in Bible class. Pull them out when you hear a sermon. Pull them out each time you sit down and read something out of the Bible. These are application words.

Just a side note here: if during the Sunday sermon your preacher ain't preaching the so what at the end of every sermon, then he ain't preaching. Preaching (read: sermons) ought to cover the so what so that you and I can take something home and apply it to our little lives in order to draw closer to God than we were before we sat down to listen. I didn't say go get up a petition to have the poor guy fired and run out of town. Read the foreword again about being nice. Back to Ephesians and the topic of Bible study.

You will notice that in Ephesians, the writer spends the first three chapters setting some truths up for the reader. He spends the rest of the book applying them to our lives. Great pattern, because we've got to know the *Who* before we know the *what*. Just learning *what* to do does little good in the long run if we don't know *Who* it is that we are following. In fact, this is the main reason we began with a long reading about the life of Jesus and the early church.

After Ephesians, go where you will. Just stay in the New Testament and stay out of Revelation and Hebrews and Jude. I know, I know, some of you are chomping at the dead cat to get at Revelation, but it isn't time. I also am very aware that some religious groups think that there are only two books of the Bible and those would be Revelation and Daniel. Those two books ARE closely related, but let's shelve them for another time, later on in this book.

OK, I shelved Revelation (and by association, Daniel), but why put the squashitus on Hebrews and Jude? Simply because they were written with the presupposition (remember those?) that the reader was well acquainted with the Old Testament--both history and law--and will not make full sense without the understanding of the first two-thirds of the Bible. Now mind you, they will make pretty good sense without the knowledge of the Law of Moses and subsequent history, but they will fall far, far short of reaching their full potential for the reader if this little bit of God's Word isn't understood.

Keep in mind some very key pointers when you are reading through the rest of the New Testament. In fact this first one is the first of the Six Rules of Interpretation: note who is speaking (or writing) and who is being spoken (or written) to. In our finishing of the New Testament letters, is one writer writing to one individual or to an entire city or church? Are there, in reality, several writers giving guidance and input (compare the opening verse of First Corinthians with the opening verse of Second Corinthians)? Are the recipients specific, or does the writer intend for this letter to be passed around at any time (see Colossians 4:16 and First Thessalonians 5:17)?

The next question one should ask is the *why* question, which is different from the *so what*. No writer, including this one, ever sat down to write just to hear the keys clack on the computer. Back when the Bible was being written, their computers were way more primitive than we have today (Apple-less society), so their writing was, indeed, a great undertaking what with all that scratching on papyrus or animal skins with rudimentary ink pens. So, they didn't write just to write. The question to be asked is *why?*

One can see readily that First Corinthians was written because the church in Corinth had problems. I count seventeen different problems, one of which was that some didn't believe in the resurrection of the dead when Jesus comes back! You may find more or less problems in your endeavor. Philemon is easy to take apart as far as *why*, also.

James? Well, there were several reasons that one was written. This is why you need that Big Chief Tablet and a sharp pencil, so you can write this stuff down as you find it. Answer the *why* and quite a surprising amount of information will be unfolded for you and placed right in your lap.

Theologians and other high powered thinkers call this kind of stuff *Occasion and Purpose of Writing*. OK, call it that if you want to. I did in one of my books. It's just easier for the common man (or woman!) to call it the *why something was written*. Is the writer answering questions and clearing up problems (like First Corinthians)? Is the writer trying to stop a feud (like the two sisters in Philippians)? Is the writer trying to get some folks back on track (like James and some of the church letters in Revelation chapters 2 & 3--oops! Sorry!

The Bible Survival Manual:

Don't go there just now)? W*hy, why, why?*--and it begins to unfold even more.

Let's close this section. If you would like, you can finish reading the New Testament (except Revelation--no, no, NO! Not yet...and Hebrews and Jude) at this point. Just do two things: place a marker after this page, and remember where you put the book! The next section contains some further reading helps that have to do with the Old Testament more than the New.

# Further Hints for Effective Reading

Let us start this section with two Parables of Pachydermic Proportion.

Both of these parables begin with two illustrations involving a room, an elephant and a group of men. The first we are familiar with, for it is the time honored story of the blind men describing an elephant. One comes up with a rough feeling snake, another a trunk of a tree and yet another a large leathery feeling leaf. Still another two long, bony feeling, yet smooth projections. Let's leave the blind fellows as they give their elephant a rub down and head across town to the scene of a crime.

The second illustration finds a room full of detectives. A man lies flat on the floor--very flat and very dead! It appears that he has been run over by a steam roller, yet the question remains how could the steam roller get in and out of the room? They poke and push trying to get close to the man but are unable. Someone yells out, "Hey, if we could get this elephant out of the way, we could get some work done!"

The first illustration is, of course, not getting the full story. The second is, of course, being oblivious to the obvious. For the most part, Bible understanding can fall in one or both of these ruts pretty quickly--and stay there for years, or perhaps a lifetime. Remember ruts? We have questions concerning the Bible. Can we understand it? Can we have our own opinions to its meaning? Can two people agree on the message?

For most Bible questions, if we avoid the pair of pitfalls of the pachydermic parables we will have a heads up. We must get the full picture and we must not practice the passover on

The Bible Survival Manual:

the obvious. Jesus, quoting from Psalm 82, said, "You are all gods." Is it true? Can we take that statement and pronounce divinity on each other? Well, some groups have, but at the expense of the other 99 & 44/100% of the Scriptures. Let's try another one:

God said, "Thou shalt not covet" and you can find that one in the Big Ten carved on the tablets of stone. Did He mean under some conditions? Was this a Jewish thing? What amendments or changes has this undergone since Mount Sinai? Obviously, God didn't want people 3500 years ago to covet--period! But what of us today? Did the cross of Christ make any difference on this matter? Can we sing and give on Sunday and covet on Monday?

What are we after in this section of study? Simple. Jesus said, "You shall know the truth and the truth shall make you free" in John 8:32. We know, without stretching the verse outside of its context, four distinct truths:

1. There is a truth
2. The truth is reality and has the capability of saving
3. The saving capability of truth isn't enacted unless one knows that truth
4. We both *can* and *should* come to understand that truth

To begin with, I believe that this one verse gives us a bit more than a promise, though great is that promise! It gives us a challenge. Jesus is giving us the gauntlet, so to speak, of our responsibility with the truth of God's Word and can be found in the last two items of our little syllogistically derived list above.

I wish it were the case that we could somehow become divinely infused with all of God's will as soon as we come to Him. I wish it were as easy as simply sleeping with the Bible as a pillow for a few nights--or even a few months--and we could somehow fully receive, fully understand, and fully be able to implement His will in our day to day rat killing. Yes, I wish, but nowhere in Scripture is that promise even hinted at. Let's pick up with a verse in John that we have discussed before and can now build just a bit more understanding on how to view and use it, as we continue in the discussion of becoming divinely infused with the will of God.

We would like to go to places such as John 14:26 and state that the one verse does (are you there, yet?), indeed, give mankind such a promise as described above. However, even though some have claimed such a promise for themselves, we need to look at this verse rather carefully. Besides, this is one of the first 'field trips' as it were, that we will take. We can now use what we have learned thus far in critically reviewing this one verse. Of course, we begin by re-reading John 14:26!

I would think that the place we would want to start would be with the context. Next, we would want to see just who is speaking and who is being spoken to. Then, there is that little item called 'occasion and purpose' that we would want to include in our decoding of this promise. We will list, then, what we have gained from asking these questions.

1. Jesus was speaking, and He was speaking to His appointed apostles.
2. The occasion was Jesus trying to get them ultimately lined up for His upcoming crucifixion, burial, resurrection--and ultimate return to the Father.
3. Specifically, Jesus gave the apostles a two-fold promise:
   - The Helper would teach them, specifically, all things; &
   - The Helper would remind them, specifically, of all things Jesus had already shared with them over the three-plus years they were together

Now, my analytical mind begins to whiz and whir and categorize and logically try to come up with what that verse might mean to me, not to the apostles standing about. I come up with...nothing.

Nothing?

I hope as I did this little exercise that you were doing one yourself. This is exactly what this book is attempting to get folks to do. I also hope that you didn't come to the same conclusion of 'nothing' that I placed on paper, for 'nothing' could be farther from the truth! 'Nothing' would have tossed the baby out with the bath water! For sure, this verse in John

The Bible Survival Manual:

14:26 is not meant to be pulled from its context and applied all over the place to everyone in every time zone. Too much of that has gone on in the name of Christianity--and the world is both watching and laughing at us. But this verse is meant to tell us something. Now just what would that something be?

**Reliability!** Look again at what Jesus is promising to Matthew, James, Andrew, Simon, Philip, Thomas, and the rest of the twelve apostles. Jesus made the promise to Judas Iscariot, but he chose not to hang around and finish his ministry. What Jesus promised was that after He went back to the Father, the apostles would be inspired in both what they said and what they wrote. I don't know about you, but that lets me know that what I read in the pages of my Bible is the truth. Jesus promised.

So, it is really too bad that we can't cash directly in on that promise. The apostles got their knowledge by inspiration and we get ours by perspiration! They listened to Jesus and got reminded along the way. We study and read and strain to remember. It is part of our growing process, but one last look at the little process we went through to understand this truism.

Time to hammer home what we have seen so far. We begin by reading. Not just reading a verse here and there off some cute daily calendar or daily devotional booklet or--gasp!-- some icebox magnet and calling it good, but sitting down and reading big blocks of Scripture. While we are reading, we have a notepad to write our questions down. Never mind that I bought stock in the Big Chief Tablet company, they are handy things to have when you read.

After reading, we ask ourselves questions concerning occasion, context, purpose, folks involved, problems, yes anything that will help us decide what is going on and what God wants us to get out of this section of Scripture. We have read after dismissing all Propprecids, and we identified all figurative language and idioms. We also have not mixed up our Bible time with the local gym. If you want to get into shape, then go jump rope at the gym. Don't jump to conclusions while reading the Bible!

As we have discussed before, the Old Testament is a bit harder to keep up with who is speaking and who is being spoken to--or even about. Take the case of Isaiah chapter 14. Read verse 12 only--reverting back to no context, just for a moment as an illustration! See if you don't find a pretty familiar name used in that verse. Some versions use the name *Light Bearer*, others *Daystar* or even *Bright Morning Star* and some, like the King James Version, use the name *Lucifer* (which is Latin for *Light Bearer*...). OK, here's the million dollar question: who is Isaiah talking about?

Many want to jump up and yell, "Satan!" at this point, for that is a name for Satan they have heard all their life, starting with Sunday school when they were a child. You're already sniffing a mouse, I'm sure. Look at the passage again, but this time expanding up and down to catch the context (meaning verses 1-23!). Who is Isaiah pointing the prophecy towards? Where in that passage did Isaiah jump track and begin talking about the Devil? At this point, honestly arrive at a conclusion of who is speaking (easy: God through Isaiah) and who is being spoken to, or being prophesied about?

For sure, a preconception, long held belief, misinterpretation, and a host of other items may have just hit the floor, since verses such as 4 and 22 clearly ascribe this to the King of Babylon, the place that the children of God would soon spend seventy years in captivity. That was the sole intent of looking at that passage, armed with the tools of Bible study we have placed in our arsenal thus far. Let's move into another arena, especially hard in the Old Testament, and that is the question: *is it true?*

Ho'boy! I can hear the pitchforks being sharpened and the torches being dipped in oil even as I type! Did I just say that we should try to pick out what is true in the Bible and what is, perhaps, an untruth? Maybe even an outright lie?

**Yes, I did** (as I quietly get up and lock my door)! Bear with me for a bit, put down the pitchforks and torches, and lemme 'splain. First of all, I believe that the Bible is the inspired word of God. If it says it happened, then it happened. If the Bible says that so-and-so--regardless of whether they were a prophet, priest or king--said such-and-such, **then they said it.** My question, however, is what they said true or a lie? Entirely a differing set of circumstances at this point. If your blood is still boiling, your teeth up, and your hackles still set

The Bible Survival Manual:

on edge, please re-read this paragraph until you get what I'm getting at. Please.

Much of what is written in the story part (largest part) of the Old Testament is without commentary. In other words, the writer is simply chronicling that, indeed, the person said/did this or that. The writer, nine times out of eight, doesn't state whether or not the person was being truthful or even what the person did was, or was not, approved by God. Take the case of Jephthah found in Judges chapter 11. If that story, along with all of the minute details isn't firmly etched in your understanding, then take the time here to read that little tragic story.

Note that the writer didn't say whether or not God approved of Jephthah's carrying out of his vow. We have a tendency to automatically think that since the story is *in the Bible* coupled with the fact that this father made *a vow to the Lord*, that somehow God was pleased with one person sacrificing his child in the name of God!

I've heard my share of preachers try to equate this story with Abraham and Isaac found in Genesis chapter 22. I've even heard pastors try to equate this story with some type of shadow of Jesus' sacrifice on the cross. I've heard a myriad of folks try to somehow, some way, wrangle this story so that it has a God-approved stamp on it. When asking the 'why do we do this' question, we see that it comes back to a belief that 'if it is in the Bible, it must be God approved.' The world listens to our apologies in cases like this, and laughs at us.

Well, Cain beat his brother to death back in Genesis chapter four and that certainly wasn't God approved. Sure, we have God getting on to Cain immediately afterwards, but do we need to have a stamp of approval--or a condemnation-- every time something is recorded for us as having been either said or done? No, we need to pull out our Bible study/Bible ciphering tools while we read and stay out of the pitfalls we have investigated and placed in our arsenal.

Just a side trip here before we leave Jephthah's story. One might well ask how someone could keep a vow like he did, when it was his daughter that came out to greet him. Surely he had a goat or a lamb or an ox in mind, not his own daughter! Why then, could someone become so blinded that he would-- *could*--carry out such a tragic end?

Personally, I believe that the answer to that query is found in verse 3 of Judges chapter 11. Reminds me of the warning found in First Corinthians 15:33, which has always been true. Yep, put a sane man and a donkey in the closet together, shut the door for two weeks, and when you open the door--out will spring two jack-asses!

Let's try another instance out of the Old Testament as we move into the prophets themselves (meaning what they wrote) or stories concerning the prophets. Take for instance, in regards to the latter, the story of Micaiah.

Take the time to read the story found in First Kings chapter 22. If you have my third book, *A Healthy Thing...Should Look Like This!*, you'll remember I devoted an entire chapter to Micaiah, who is one of my favorites when it comes to character. Notice in the Bible that Zedekiah confronts Micaiah and wonders, out loud (right after he slaps Micaiah), just "when did the Spirit of God jump from me to you?" Keep in mind that Ahab's prophets had prophesied one thing and Micaiah prophesied another (you did read the story, didn't you?). After reading their respective prophecies, both cannot be right!

The reasonable explanation is that Ahab's prophets were telling Ahab what he wanted to hear. I know that is a foreign concept to our overarching honest society today, but believe you me it used to go on! Yes, please pardon my sarcasm and back to Micaiah. There is overwhelming internal evidence in the story that what Micaiah was prophesying was from God and what Zedekiah and his cronies were prophesying was fabricated, even though it isn't specifically spelled out in the text by the one writing the story.

Again, it is true that Zedekiah, *et.al.*, said those things. It is not true that what they said was true. That should clear it up. If not, again: Zedekiah truly said some things that truly weren't true. He lied. OK.

I'm not trying to set everyone out on a witch hunt through the Bible finding this little untruth or that little fabrication. What I am trying to get across is that if the story or the statement sounds a little confusing or seems to go against the God you have come to know, then go back and reread the story or statement again, within its context and other parameters, and see if it just might not fall into this realm we've been discussing.

The Bible Survival Manual:

Again, we will call this realm: just because someone said it or did it, doesn't guarantee that this was something that was God approved--it just might be the writer recording that someone said it or did it.

A note before we leave this section. I have read, reread, reworded, reworked and fretted over this section many, many hours. It is my dying hope that this section was far more of a help than it was a hindrance or stumbling block. Any *How To* book wouldn't be complete without touching on this subject, precarious though it may be. Let's take a break and cover a subject that won't be controversial at all.

Well, I guess anything could be controversial if you find the right two people, so on to the next roundup!

# Take a Breather!

Let's take the time for a bit of review to see where we've come and see if there is anything left to bite off and chew on. [I bet he finds something!] To begin with, we saw in the Foreword the reason for yet another Bible study book. As long as man misuses the Bible, there is a need for a How To book. Besides, it would be the exception--not the rule--if God personally told you all the information He intends for you to know.

We then waded through some of my **Presuppositions** that, I believe, have held up throughout this book. These particular Presuppositions looked a bit like some rules of interpretation discussed later, but they are helpful by themselves. We discovered that the Bible is inspired, but not 'faxed' down from Heaven word-for-word. The Bible is also in a form that each one of us can read and understand--and it is void of the so-called 'decoder-ring-hidden-messages' that some people crave.

We moved on and dealt with **Context** and noted that it is everything when it comes to passages, phrases or individual verses in the Bible. Without Context, it is ever so easy to make a pretext. Pretexts are a left hand turn when one ought to be traveling straight ahead.

**Conclusions** were visited next. The greatest lesson on conclusions, when all the dust was settled from all of the words written about them, is to simply not jump to any until the different passages and entries in the Bible are read *and* understood. Jumping to a conclusion based upon a single verse found in one lone entry of the Bible is dangerous ground indeed! This is where koo-koo nuts come from!

Through **Understanding *Your* Bible's Origin...English-wise** we gained insight into how this Book of books came from the original languages of antiquity into something that we can all read and understand, focusing on the English language. Though versions and translations would be discussed farther along, we grabbed a little wisdom into just why it is that folks use the particular Bible that they do and found that there usually isn't any Great Theological Reason--just preference. We also hit the greatest warning of them all when it comes to versions: staying out of the Version Wars.

**Bible Readability** almost didn't make it into this book. Part of the Bible Readability problem rests in simply finding a big enough print or going and buying some reading glasses so that one can actually see the words! Because of pride or being downright cheap, many folks I have known have forgone reading the Bible. Please, get the print size right so you can spend some time with God. If it isn't the size of the print, but the size of the words that is stalling you, then get a Bible you can read!

The remainder of Readability was spent on the varying translations or versions. There are the basic two camps--D-E & F-E--of English Bibles to choose from. Within these two camps there are dozens of Bibles to choose from. We did discuss the need of not becoming so glued to one that you, as a Bible reader, do not avail yourself of several different translations across the two differing camps. Something long hidden to you may come alive because you practiced this as a routine.

Finally, when it comes to versions, don't let anyone downplay you simply because you use one version or another. You don't necessarily have to hit them (not necessarily!), just either ignore them or try to teach them out of their error. All versions are good. All have mistakes here and there, but none so hideous as to keep one out of Heaven!

**The Six Rules of Interpretation** were hit upon next, with a strong hint to write down these six rules onto one of the little blank pages in every Bible for a handy reference later on while reading or studying. These six rules contain the meat of the matter, so to speak, when it comes to Bible understanding. If a blank page cannot be had, a sticky note will suffice. If these rules of interpretation are followed, quite a huge chunk of Scripture will be unfolded into your lap--and weird Christianity can be averted.

Next, we discussed **Preparing for Bible Study**. And why not? We prepare for everything else in life--including the daily routines--why should our Bible study time be any different? The preparation can (and should) range from the simple acts of discarding the distractions around us, to bolstering our knowledge of the life and times of the people we are reading about.

One of the best overall items we can include in our preparation to study the Bible is to get into the habit of asking the Author of the Bible any of the various questions that will wash over us while reading and studying. If we run to the head honcho at our local church building, we will become simply mini-honchos. Wouldn't it be far, far greater to become a little like God instead? We have lost the art of waiting upon the Lord as a people. You can be part of the new awakening and reverse that process.

**Propprecids** was the next stop. This mnemonic tip stood for prejudice, opinions and preconceived ideas which are always, always a bad item when one is trying to study the Bible and gain from it life changing ideas. Though the prejudice we're speaking of doesn't necessarily need to be in the racial hatred arena that we usually place it in, it oftentimes bleeds over into that awful area.

The opinions and preconceived ideas usually manifest themselves into a wrongfully held--but long held--belief that the Bible states this or that, when in fact it doesn't! Yes, it can be as benign as placing the 'three wise men' around the manger every Christmas season, or it can be a complete missing of the mark on a Bible teaching. When we dutifully dump the Propprecids each and every time we come to the Bible, we stand a greater chance of gaining a bit more ground in our quest for God.

In the section **Reading the Bible**, we got into the actual 'how to' arena of just where to start and where to go in this great endeavor. We discussed that the Bible is sixty-six separate entries spanning many centuries. To simply sit down and read the Bible from cover to cover will certainly get the job done, but it may not be the best plan of attack!

Since the Bible is a book centered on Jesus as the Savior of the world, it is best to start with the first five books of the New

Testament that tell the story of both the Christ, and the church He came to earth to build.

A pair of Pachydermic parables introduced the **Further Hints for Effective Reading**. If anyone was going to fall by the wayside in this little book, this would be the place! If this book were an onion (and I know it has brought tears to some folks' eyes!), then this section is, in reality, peeling another layer off and getting deeper into Bible study and reading. This is the section that calls us to pay ever so close attention to especially the rule of interpretation concerned with who is speaking and who is being spoken to.

We saw in this section that not every promise or curse found in the Bible is necessarily directed at us two-thousand plus years down the road. We also discovered that there just might be some items and stories in the Bible that are simply not true. Yes, yes, the person may have actually said the words, but what the person said was not true. Same with actions: just because someone did whatever they did, it doesn't mean that God approved of their actions *simply because it is recorded in the Bible!*

I do wish to throw this little speed bump into the book at this point: if this chapter on Further Hints did not quite ring with you, or didn't quite make sense to you, please take a little break if you need to then come back and reread the chapter. I promise you it will make sense if you give it a go. It isn't necessarily easy, but it is important. Too many mistakes have been made out in Interpretation/Application Land because these principles were violated. Some mistakes have been grand in scale.

I believe we have caught up. Yes, there are two more items that I wish to share with you before this book closes. You may want to think about the point here at which we find ourselves as the ending of **Bible Course 101** and the beginning of **Bible Course 102**, this chapter being the 'review' for the final exam of *Bib101*. No, there isn't a test with this book. Oh, there's a test alright, but I'm not the one giving it. The test will be a self-examination as you sit down with God's Word from now on.

And don't despair if you find yourself slogging through this book. You have a lifetime to read and refer back here as many times as you would like or need. That was the design and intent when I started this work. Much more important than delving into, and fighting with, this book is the time spent with God's Word for you.

Now, for *Bib102*...

The Bible Survival Manual:

# Common Bible Threads

As stated earlier in this book, the main theme of the Bible is Jesus Christ. Without God coming down to earth in the form of us, we could never really relate to Him. We know this by hindsight, but before He came, mankind just simply could not have grasped this concept. God, since He is God, knew this in advance. That is why very early on in your Bible, Adam and Eve are given the promise of a Savior.

Indeed, Jesus being the central theme of the entire Bible was the driving impetus in our choosing to read the Bible in the order that we did: first five books of the New Testament first. However, there is another common thread or theme in the Bible that I wish to leave you with in your quest for a deeper study. It is a thread that weaves through both the Old and the New Testament.

The Old Testament is generally taken up with God's laws for the Jewish nation, and the subsequent prophets who tried to keep them, or bring them back, in line. Genesis isn't along these lines. It wasn't until the Jews received the Ten Commandments that they were headed to becoming a nation. God wanted the Jews out of Egyptian slavery and into the Promised Land for a reason: God wanted the Jews to be the physical lineage by which Jesus came into the world. This is why they are referred to as the Chosen People of God. They were simply chosen to be the ones by which Messiah came into the world. They were not chosen to go to Heaven any more than you and I are based upon human parameters and markers. No one gets to automatically enter Heaven simply because of their race or the color of their skin. I know that's a shock to some white supremacy groups, but it is the truth.

When Jesus came to earth, He came on two distinct

missions. The first and foremost of these missions was to show all of mankind the way to Heaven. The second mission was to fulfill the Law of Moses (that the Jews had been living under for centuries) and thereby nullifying it, nailing it to the cross so to speak. He accomplished both by living a sinless life and sacrificing His life so that we don't have to. Once fulfilled, it is no longer valid and binding for anyone.

However, whether you are reading along in the Old Testament about the Law of Moses the Jews were (supposed to be) living under, or you are reading along in the New Testament about how all of mankind is (supposed) to be living, there are a couple of common items, sub-threads if you will. One of these items is centered on how God wants us to view Him and the other is how God wants us to view our fellow man.

It is pretty evident in reading Genesis chapter three that God really doesn't appreciate folks lying to Him and trying to play the blame game, as Adam and Eve did after munching the fruit in the talking snake incident. The very next chapter shows us that God expects us to treat others as well as we treat ourselves. No, you can't kill your own brother just because you're hacked and pouty. Throughout the rest of the Old Testament, God continuously comes down hard, by way of judgment, on folks that don't treat other folks well--especially when those folks being mistreated are the poor, defenseless or downtrodden in society. In short, folks that cannot help themselves.

Then we come into the New Testament and find the same lessons about our fellow man being taught. Multiple times during Jesus' ministry the correct answer to the question of 'what might the greatest commandment from Moses be' was answered with 'loving God with everything one has, and loving one's neighbor as himself.' It was even pointed out in Jesus' day that this simple answer was the hook that the entirety of the Law of Moses and the prophets' messages hinged on, keeping in mind that the Law and the prophets were the core of the mind of God.

Even the Big Ten, the Ten Commandments, can be divided equally in half on the above point. The first five of the commandments have to do with man and God and the last

The Bible Survival Manual:

five have to do with a man to man relationship. Take a look at them. It would seem to not be divided 50/50 at first glance, but think about them for a while and see if it doesn't become clear.

Take a look at the prophet Micah's writing. It's OK if you have to hit the table of contents in your Bible to find it. When you do, then go to chapter six. If you would like, you could read all of the prophet in order to set the context, but I'll save you some time as I make this next point.

God is angry with the people of the Promised Land. Why? Mostly because they had been doing some of the things I mentioned above, disregarding their fellow man or even stomping him while he was down. God decides to take them to court so they can plead their case of why they have been acting like spiritual knuckleheads. He's going to give them all the time they need to plead their case to the mountains--or anything else that will listen! Then, God tells them what He has wanted from them all this time.

No, He didn't want a sacrifice. Not even a VERY HUGE sacrifice! What God wanted out of His people is found in Micah 6:8:

*He has told you, O man, what is good and what the Lord requires of you: to do justice, to love kindness, and to walk humbly with your God.*

Now, mind you, this was written many centuries before Jesus walked the earth. Sounds a bit like the 'love God, and love your fellow man like yourself' we discussed above, doesn't it? Indeed, it IS the same for that is what God has required of mankind all along. Therefore, when you read along in the Bible, keep this idea in mind. You will certainly come away with the conclusion that, even though the Testaments have changed, God never changed!

Here is where we introduce another common sub-thread throughout the Bible. If God wants all people's hearts throughout all of history, then how is it that we are to connect up with Him in the first place? That answer is found in the Old Testament prophecy of Habakkuk, in chapter two, verse four: *the righteous will live by faith.*

Now, I'm really hoping that all you graduates of **Bib101**

Mystifying to Manageable

are jumping up and down right about now yelling, "You just gave us a verse! Where's the context?!" Ah, very good! See, *Bib101* was well worth the time and money you put into it! [Watch, he's gonna wriggle] Allow me a bit of time and space to point something out before we continue on with our subject. No, I'm not wriggling, I'm teaching! By stating that the answer was found in Habakkuk 2:4, I'm simply stating that the phrase *the righteous will live by faith* is found in that verse. You are correct in balking at just pulling something from one verse and calling it good. Allow me a paragraph of digression for the sake of review. Review is good.

Take the time to read enough of Habakkuk to garner the context--if for no other reason than to prove, or disprove, what I just stated. The first two chapters ought to be enough. Note that the last chapter is a separate occasion and purpose. It is a prayer for the people. Chapters one and two are a back-and-forth dialogue between God and the prophet. By the time we get to Habakkuk 2:4, you have already noted that it is now God speaking, and He's letting the prophet in on some of the ways that He thinks!

You may be musing in the back of your mind, wondering just why am I here in some Old Testament Minor Prophet (by the way, they are called Minor because of length, not content) when Jesus, and His words of salvation, are in the New Testament. Here is why: that one particular verse found in Habakkuk was important enough to God, that He made sure it was quoted three times in the New Testament! In fact, you may have these references already in your margin notes for Habakkuk 2:4.

Take the time to examine Galatians 3:11, Romans 1:17, and Hebrews 10:38. Yes, one should take the time to examine the context and see why the various New Testament writers were referencing an Old Testament prophet who wrote some six-hundred years before they were even born. Galatians and Romans were written by the Apostle Paul, but Hebrews was written by--someone else, but definitely not Paul! Though the author of Hebrews isn't mentioned, it isn't Paul. How do I know?

The same way you can tell that the annoying anonymous letter which was slipped under your door at home last

The Bible Survival Manual:

Saturday was not written in any shape, form or fashion by your Aunt Mabel! Aunt Mabel doesn't use those words and doesn't construct her sentences like that. It might have been written or typed by your mean old boss at work, but Aunt Mabel? No, no, no!

That was a side-rant, but to show that two different writers of the New Testament continued to pull the thread of living by faith up through the remainder of the Bible. But how can the concept of *living by faith* be pulled along throughout the Bible if Jesus came to fulfill and, subsequently, nullify the old Law of Moses, thereby ushering in a new covenant with mankind? Two words: grounds and means.

The *grounds* for a saving relationship with God <u>has always been</u> and <u>will always be</u>, **Faith In God**, however, the *means* by which faith connects up with mankind changed with the teachings, death, burial and resurrection of Jesus Christ. Take as many passes at that last sentence as you need in order to fully bring it in and understand it. Much, including a continuous understanding while doing Bible reading and studying, depends on this concept. This will answer the question raised as to why many items taught in the Old Testament, as part of the Law given at Mount Sinai when Moses received the Big Ten, look quite a bit like many of the teachings of Jesus as in the Sermon on the Mount in Matthew. Faith in God has always been the *grounds* for man connecting back to God. Only the means changed one Friday afternoon on a cross outside Jerusalem.

However, Jesus nullified the Big Ten (by fulfilling the Law), along with all of the sacrifices and feasts that man was required to keep in obedience to God, and *aren't you glad?!* I, for one, would not want to keep bunches of goats and rams in my back yard, hauling them across the ocean to the temple for a sacrifice several times a year. No, I'm forever grateful that Jesus came to enact a 'better way,' if I may borrow from Hebrews 7:22 & 8:6!

Hopefully, this will assist you in keeping the covenants straight while you are reading and studying your way through the Bible, Old and New Testaments alike. This is in no ways an in-depth treating of this subject. We can, in no way, delve into the idea that in God's plan, Jesus was crucified before the foundations of the world even though He was crucified in a

## Mystifying to Manageable

point in historical time. Think of this whole chapter up to this point as being more like one of those sixty second trailers for an action flick. Just enough to let you know that the movie will be one of those really swell action, blow-em-up, high speed guy flicks instead of one of those drizzling love stories where bunches of dour, glum folks sit around and discuss their feelings for two hours.

---

That was pretty much it for ***Bib102***. Short, but deep. As this is unfolding on my computer, it is scarcely five pages long compared with nearly seventy-five for ***Bib101***. However, there is much in ***Bib102*** that needs to be taken in...*especially before preceding to the next section!* This cannot be over stressed. Yes, the next section...

Even as I am sitting here typing these words, pondering the next section, I am developing Belshazzar's Disease, which can be found described in Daniel 5:6- "Then the king's countenance was changed, and his thoughts troubled him, so that the joints of his hips went slack, and his knees smote one against another."

In fact, if you would like, you can call it good right here after completing both ***Bib101*** and ***Bib102***, and you will have completed the vast majority of what I set about to accomplish. Anything after this point will be considered **Extra Credit**. Just like in school, extra credit is not required. No one will look down on you or ostracize you in any way, shape or fashion if you close the book right here.

No, don't throw the book away. It is designed to be referenced throughout your lifetime or to be used to teach others.

The next section has to do with using our heads. One may call it an appeal to common sense. There is just one thing about the idea of common sense that should bug us, and that is... well, just read the following quotes about common sense and we shall have laid the groundwork for the caveat:

• On common sense and education, Tom Heehler stated, "The more you think you have of one, the less you think you need of the other."

The Bible Survival Manual:

- Albert Einstein rightly said concerning most of it, "Common sense is nothing more than a deposit of prejudices laid down by the mind before you reach eighteen."
- Lastly, Stuart Chase summed it up with, "Common sense is that which tells us the world is flat."

So, why would I want to launch off into a section of extra credit centered around the notion of common sense? What would make me believe that a section based upon an immeasurable item would add to our Biblical knowledge, instead of creating thin ice whereby the whole of *Bib101* & *Bib102* could come crashing down? What would--or even possibly could--make me believe I could skate out from under the fulfilling of the above three curse-quotes?

By all probabilities, (like every other human on the planet) I believe I possess common sense enough to pull it off. Well, I also believe that I'm a babe magnet and that I look just as good as I did the day I graduated from high school! However, and more believable, I also strongly think that if a person has digested and understood all of the helps, hints and how-to's strung throughout this book (especially the one about the cycle of communication with God), they possess enough common sense to plow ahead into a section about common sense.

So, with that in mind, let's have a go at it, shall we? [He's scaring me!]

# Cranial Muscle

There are several items that (should!) set us apart from the animal kingdom. Yes, yes, I know that we are classified *in* the animal kingdom but that doesn't mean we should act like animals! For an example, I don't sit around grooming others. When I go out to coffee, I do not pick the lice and ticks off of the other people in my group and pop them in my mouth. In fact, I usually don't let others do that to me, either. I don't witness anyone else in any other group grooming, so I hope I don't step on some toes here. This is one of many things that set us apart from animals such as sheep, slugs, oarfish and chimps.

Another item that (should!) set us apart from the animal kingdom is our cranial muscle, also known as the brain. In short, we can think and animals can't. For sure, the dog and cat lovers who are reading this are pretty much wanting to fry me right now, but hear me out for a few lines.

I'm thinking (pun *intended!*) that a cat cannot weigh two issues that have ramifications set far in the future, then set about making plans which may take weeks or years to accomplish, thereby obtaining one goal at the expense of the other. A dog cannot sit down with a set of instructions, decide if he has all the parts, then build even so much as a lean-to shelter half out of Lincoln logs. A goldfish can't...well...do anything! THAT's what I mean by the word *think*. Yes, they're all cute, and honest, and all of the other anthropomorphisms we lay on them, but they can't do what we do. We are unique. We are God designed.

God made us as thinking individuals. God expects us to use our brains in this life, and even use said brains when we come to the Bible. Huh? What? How can I make such a statement as that? Worth exploring, as I further lay a foundation for this extra credit section.

The Bible Survival Manual:

In Luke chapter ten, Jesus is once more being heckled by the religious leaders of His day. They never let up, all the way to, and including, the cross. One lawyer, who was just certain that he could trap Jesus, asked Jesus a question concerning eternal life: what does someone have to do to inherit it? After asking the question, the Lawyer probably clapped his hands, wrested a little smile, and busted a quick move with his feet under cover of his long, flowing robe. In verse twenty-six, Jesus answers the lawyer by counter-questioning him (with both barrels, I might add!) with, "What is written in the Law? How does it read to you?"

The lawyer saw that counter-questioning worked pretty well so he thought he would try a bit of it himself (after correctly answering the Master) and asked the Christ just who his neighbor might be. Jesus gives him six verses worth of a story, then asks the Lawyer a very stinging question to which the Lawyer correctly answers and promptly fades from view! I would have done the same if I were him, but let's examine just what went on in this series of questions and counter-questions.

Jesus was asking the Lawyer to put on his thinking cap. First, He asked the Lawyer to dip back into what we call the Old Testament and come up with an intelligent answer. Then, Jesus told him a little story and asked him to draw a conclusion based upon both the contents of the story and the teachings from the Old Testament.

If you wish, there is plenty of material floating around out there on the subjects of abductive, inductive, analogical and deductive reasoning. For our purposes, we will lump all of these together and call it the *ability to think*. What we will be trying to avoid is the little item called fallacious reasoning. Yep, that's a big, fancy term for *thinkin' about sumpin' and comin' up with garbage*. It happens all the time to the best of us, and it seems to have happened along the way when it comes to Bible reading, also. But, where does it come from when we are discussing the latter?

To begin with, by and large, it comes when those help items mentioned in **Bib101** & **Bib102** are not understood, taken to heart and applied. Remember our little illustration of the person who simply looks up First Kings 11:9 and then makes up their mind that God is that way all the time in all circumstances? Of course, we would think that is pretty silly, but it happens all the time. Not too long ago I was looking at some comments posted under some Christian worship videos on the internet. Both the nay-sayers and the defenders were doing the never-ending battle with postings, but it was very apparent, among much of what was written, that Rule of Interpretation #4 had been side stepped.

Then, we should remember all of the collective discussions about the baggage we bring to the table, wrapped up in the Propprecids. These can't be overstressed as to the amount of damage and 'missing of the mark' these can produce, especially when it comes to isogesis. Again, isogesis is when we come to the Bible with our minds made up about a particular subject, then scrounge around in the concordance till we find a verse that we can 'make' prove our point of view. This has done untold damage in the arena of Bible knowledge. In fact, it has done untold damage simply in the arena of Christianity.

However, the Bible *is* and *will remain* a book that mankind is intended to put a little brain grease into. As we discussed before, if the Bible were laid out like an auto manual it would be a different story. If God had simply faxed some rules and regulations down out of Heaven in an indexed and categorized fashion, we wouldn't be having this discussion. When someone *taught* something wrong, *thought* something wrong or *did* something wrong, we could simply look it up in the index and state to the person, "You have committed an infraction on Section IV, Paragraph 18, Rule #8," and begin singing *Just As I Am*, while we watch the wretched individual slither down the aisle the next Sunday morning.

Oh, wait! We attempt to do this all the time!

However, the Bible isn't laid out in How-to-Fix-It-Manual mode, but in a fashion that invites each reader to come to grips with its contents, measure their life against the various conclusions mixed in, yes, amongst some hard and fast, cut and dried, commandments, then adjust their life according to their understanding *at the time*. I stress *at the time*, because we should hold the attitude of, and remain, a work in progress throughout the time God allows us to breathe air.

We should remain--not *judges* of one another--but, *helpers* of one another in our quest for understanding, knowledge, wisdom and a God shaped life. Each of us holds the responsibility to dig, wrestle, search, wrestle, read and wrestle some more with God's Will for our lives. Having written that, let us now move into a few practical exercises to illustrate what is meant by brain grease. Allow me a couple of little stories:

### The Example of Joshial:

Joshial's mind wandered as he blinked in the bright sunlight and began to stare at the markings on his knuckles. To most anyone else, the markings wouldn't mean anything. They were in plain black ink about a centimeter tall, and although he had worn them for decades, they never seemed to fade, even at his age. He could have had them removed, but something always stopped him. Joshial's mind continued to wonder--and wander...

All who processed into Dachau saw the sign, "Arbeit Macht Frei," which roughly translated "Work Empowers Freedom." Many had to strain to read it through the sides of the cattle cars. After a quick unloading, amid a torrent of shouts in any language except their own, coupled with the most rude punchings and pushing, all riders in the cattle cars were immediately separated and divided into groups based obviously upon physical size and gender. No matter what group, each received a unique set of numbers hurriedly and painfully etched deep into their knuckles. Everyone wondered if it could get any more painful than this. In a short time, they would know the answer to that question. Work set no one free.

- Nowhere do these two paragraphs state that Joshial was in Dachau.
- Nowhere do these two paragraphs state that Joshial had *numbers* tattooed on his knuckles.
- We know Joshial was in Dachau and still had the identification tattoo that the Schutzstaffel put on him because we have brains!

## Mystifying to Manageable

Or...can we safely state all of the above? Can we state it in such a way as to embed it in stone for all of eternity? This becomes the meat of the matter in this Extra Credit section, as we discuss being able to think through passages of the Bible and make conclusions. Perhaps we can state some clear items about Joshial.

To begin with, the first two bulleted items above are true. Nothing that we could read before or after these two pulled passages, which sit one after the other in the original, can possibly change these facts. The third bulleted item is the one in question. How shall we treat it? Also, is the truthfulness of the first two bulleted items enough to make both a dent and a difference? Stay with me, now!

For sure, context seems to be the overarching decider. Context usually is, this is why we confidently state earlier in this work that *context is everything*, and even began our study with it. We could certainly allow the third bulleted item to stand, unless, after reading the <u>entire</u> work we found something that would completely upend that conclusion. Perhaps we would find, upon finishing the work, something that would substantiate, or deny us, our conclusion. Consider these two alternate paragraphs that appear later in the story:

1-Joshial was early for the meeting, but he loved to sit in the small city park outside the meeting hall, for this time of the year the weather was usually most agreeable. Today, a small child sat next to him on the park bench. Joshial was unaware that the child was reading out loud the numbers from the back of his fingers, until his mother--now fully aware of what her young daughter was doing--quickly pulled on the child's arm and sharply told her to stop, out of pure embarrassment! Shortly, Joshial's fellow Dachau survivors began to emerge from the subway's underground staircase. Each year, there were less and less of them at these meetings.

2-Joshial found himself hiding once again. Yes, hiding is something that he knew well. Joshial had spent nearly five years of his young childhood hiding with first this family and then with another, moving as circumstances began to heat up

The Bible Survival Manual:

and change. He remembered the day that his father was taken away from him, never to see him again except for that quick look he had through the barbed wire cage that surrounded Dachau. He could hardly look his father in the eye that day, concentrating instead on the numbers etched deeply on his father's knuckles, which were still oozing blood. As soon as he was old enough, Joshial would have those very numbers recreated on his own knuckles, out of memory for the fate of his father.

Each paragraph above changes the game. In the first paragraph, we are allowed to keep our conclusion that Joshial was in Dachau and those, indeed, were numbers on his knuckles. In the second paragraph, only part of the conclusions we had reached we were able to keep. Yes, they were numbers on his knuckles, but we had to abandon the thought of Joshial, himself, being housed in Dachau.

Since these alternate paragraphs were placed nowhere near the original first two, we had to rely more on Rules of Interpretation #4 and #5 instead of context alone. This is to illustrate how these Rules of Interpretation work with all of the other tools we have now at our disposal. One more illustration by way of a story:

**The Example of Jack:**
With all the anger that he could focus, Jack raced up the embankment, firmly gripping his rifle and knowing that he only had four shots left. One question raced through his mind--would he have enough time?

At the top of the hill Jack knew he had a clear shot. First shot caught a fleeing one squarely between the shoulders. He didn't even so much as raise dust when he hit the ground. Jack could now only count on his ability to shoot, for time was not on his side. Second round, and the last runner rolled. They did not make the bridge.

Jack inspected the two downed objects. One was gone and the other would be soon enough. Jack slumped down, wondering what to do next...

Besides being the makings of a doggone great story, this

Mystifying to Manageable

little piece raises more questions than anything near answers. I'm sure that there could be endless possibilities of why Jack felt the need to shoot two fleeing folks in the back, who wanted desperately to reach and cross some bridge. Here are a couple:

- Jack was a soldier, trying to keep the enemy from reaching the much needed bridge and set off demolition charges. This would certainly work in many instances, however, let's explore the next one.

- Jack was a farmer, pushed to the brink by young boys looting his farm and destroying his fields. Not a very pleasant outcome for either Jack or the boys who were stealing watermelons out of Jack's truck patch!

And who said they were boys? Who said that Jack was the landowner? See how easily we get sidetracked and subsequently sideswiped?!

Jack's identity and how we view him have everything to do with the events of this story. By now, you have noted that, just like the four-letter word **tear** in our long ago illustration, we simply do not have enough context--or anything else!--to make any claims on Jack or his actions. We simply have to leave it as it is. Nothing, no nothing, can be stated further about this second illustration. Sad as that may be to you, are there any examples in the Bible like this latter one concerning Jack? [He is, for sure, going to pull something out of the Bible] Several come to my mind. [See? T-O-L-D told ya he would!]

Take a moment or two and read the curious story found in Matthew chapter twenty-seven, verses fifty through fifty-three. Read it *carefully!* Go up and down the page like a window shade, gathering as many verses before this passage, or after, that will help you establish the context. When you are satisfied you have the context, pick back up here in this book for a series of questions.

Where else in the New Testament is this story found? What other verses in the New Testament will assist you in understanding everything you are dying to know about this passage? Old Testament? Any Testament?!

The Bible Survival Manual:

For sure, Jesus giving up His spirit and the veil of the temple being torn in two from top to bottom can be found in Mark chapter fifteen and Luke chapter twenty-three (though Luke doesn't give us the direction 'top to bottom' like Matthew and Mark), but the curious story about the tombs being opened and the saints being raised to walk about while Jesus was on the cross is unique to Matthew. Oops!

If you read it carefully, you noted where I jumped ship--didn't you--at the end of the last paragraph? Scramble back if you need to read it one more time. Matthew states that the tombs of the saints were opened when the veil was being torn, but that the saints were not raised until after Jesus' resurrection, wandering the streets of Jerusalem. Yes, just a friendly reminder to always read things as close as you can.

My, oh my, that must have been one shocker of a deal there. Imagine that Aunt Mabel drops in to the Jerusalem Meat Market to buy a holiday ham. She nods and says, "Shalom," to old Ishmael who is also standing in line. The conversation might go a bit like:

"And 'Shalom' to you, Aunt Mabel, during this Passover and Pentecost season!"

"Say, didn't we bury you a couple of weeks back?"

"Yes, you did, but I'm back. I'm here because I'm very hungry right now."

"Oh, I see, well, 'Mazal Tov'to you, Ishmael."

Back to reality, it should be noted that there isn't any more that someone can say--*let alone teach!--concerning Matthew 27:52-53 than what is stated. Period!* It may not be this passage of Scripture, but I will bet you a dollar to a doughnut that you have already heard someone stand up and try to teach something on a small passage of Scripture that is 1-confusing at best, and 2-by itself in the entirety of the Bible...meaning there is nothing that will assist you from the Old Testament, and certainly nothing from the New.

Another verse just came to mind. [He does that] Again, go back and refresh yourself with Rule of Interpretation #5 and note the passage which was used as an illustration of that rule. That passage, from First Timothy chapter two, about a woman's salvation being tied to childbearing has no equal in the entire Bible. Just like our story about Jack's shooting spree and the resurrected saints in Matthew, there is no platform, whatsoever, to begin to teach *anything* about women's salvation from First Timothy 2:15, though some have tried--and tried *real hard!*

It should, therefore, be just a bit on the scary side when someone mounts a pulpit Sunday morning about ten o'clock and begins laying and hammering down 'tidbits from Heaven' on these types of verses and passages, when there is nothing one can garner from them. Be on the lookout. Use your God-given abilities to think something through. Time to head to ancient Greece and scare up Ol' Hermes.

The Bible Survival Manual:

# Hermeneutics

As the story goes, two old blue-haired sisters were visiting in the pews after Sunday school, waiting for the worship time to begin. Neither could hear well, so in their overcompensation all of those in the sanctuary were able to get in on the conversation. Mabel was asked what her new Sunday school class was about to which she replied rather loudly that it was about hermeneutics. "What did you say?" was quickly--and loudly--driven back to Mabel to which she yelled in reply, "I said *hermeneutics!*"

The entire church family was broken up with, "Who, on God's green earth, is Herman...and why should the Sunday school class be so concerned about his nootiks?" You may be asking the same question yourself! Now that we are fully armed to the teeth with common sense, let's jump in with Herman and take a look at his nootiks in three easy steps. First, a little explanation about hermeneutics, and just where did we get that word?

Hermes was the Greek god who brought messages from deity to mankind in that flavor of mythology. Put that together with the Greek word for *nodding to show direction or favor*, and you have hermeneutics--the art of bringing the meaning out of the Scriptures. This is an art that should be practiced from the pulpit each and every Sunday, without fail.

Hermeneutics comes in three steps. Step one is obviously **reading** the text. Step two is **exegesis**, with the final step being one of **application** through reason. How easy is that? Actually, armed with good Bible study skills and tools, it isn't that hard. It is just something that bears watching so that one doesn't skid off the road into the ditch. Let's look at the three steps in a few words, but first a side trip about Bible tools.

Think of your Bible as a car. You park the car in the garage.

Hanging up on the wall of the garage, or neatly categorized and tucked away in drawers, are tools. The tools are not the car, but they help get everything out of the car that you could wish. You make minor adjustments with tools, or fix something that is broken with the car. Now, in our illustration let's not push it too far.

No, the Bible doesn't need adjustments or fixing. We might (and do!) from time to time, but not the Bible. The tools are for our adjustment and alignment. Just keep in mind that study helps, references, commentaries, word study books, your minister and all else along those lines aren't the Bible. Just helps! Now, back to the steps of hermeneutics:

**Step #1: Read the text:** This excludes Hallmark reading. This excludes intermittent reading. This excludes devotional reading. This excludes study help reading. This excludes margin note hopping. This excludes Daily Breads and verses transcribed upon calendars and icebox magnets. This excludes listening to sermon tapes or watching religious television programs. This might be listening to the Bible on CD if that is your form of reading the Bible. While reading the text, keep in mind the six rules of interpretation and the bit about preparation.

**Step #2: Exegesis:** This is the art of deciding what the text meant to those who originally received it. *This is the step of the study helps we have been slogging through up till now.* You may find a simple map helpful. An encyclopedia of Bible times and customs may be helpful. An expository dictionary of Bible words may be helpful. Remember, just as important as using all of your Bible tools, is to pay attention and not bring into the picture more than your Bible tools will produce. In short, don't turn exegesis upside down and into isogesis. Remember, isogesis is making the Scriptures say what you want them to say. Bad, bad, always bad.

**Step #3: Application:** This is the step of deciding if this Scripture is moving you to either do something, stop something or think something. Oftentimes, if mistakes are made in step #2, that mistake is ballooned in this third step. If the Six rules

The Bible Survival Manual:

of Interpretation were not adhered to, then mistakes can--will--be made. [He's going to pull out an example right about now, just watch...]

Time will be well spent if we look at some examples of these three steps. [He's predictable!] We will call this first one, *Christians Are Allowed to Eat Rabbit Sandwiches.* Follow along in your Bible, so this will make sense:

You grab some cookies, a tall glass of milk and sit down to read about the food laws of the Old Testament found in Leviticus chapter 11. You are not sure what constitutes a cud chewing or split hoof animal. You do know that whatever they are, they are forbidden to be ingested according to this passage. Again, let me stress: *according to this passage.* You begin to get worried and consult a Bible dictionary, only to find out that you can't eat pigs and rabbits, since they fall into this category of animals mentioned in Leviticus chapter 11. You set down the cookies and grudgingly get up and clean out your freezer. The holiday ham Aunt Mabel bought at the Jerusalem Meat Market is the first to go. Dogs in the backyard are gracious. Many dollars worth of deli-sliced rabbit sandwich meat goes out to the now grinning dogs.

Your mistake? You violated Rule #4 of the Six Rules of Interpretation, re-created here for your convenience: *Partial truth on any one subject is only able to direct one to a conclusion. Full understanding and truth comes about when all the verses that pertain to a subject are read and considered.* Specifically, you either haven't read or have forgotten that Jesus declared all foods clean in Mark chapter 7. God reiterated that same concept when He gave Peter an object lesson, found in Acts chapter 10, of lowering the sheet full of critters specifically forbidden by Leviticus chapter 11 and asking Peter to get up and fix a sandwich. Brain grease passages, such as Colossians 2:13-15 and many others, were not figured in to your little foray at the icebox. Nobody but the dogs benefited from the wrong conclusion.

This is why, by and large, you can still find folks who are scrambling in their lives trying to recreate some type of adherence to the laws of the Old Testament. They have failed to read all there is on any one subject. They have made conclusions (and bound them on others) without the whole story. Let's look at three more that have nothing whatsoever to do with sandwiches or rabbits, but center around headgear.

**Example #2:** You read First Corinthians chapter 11 and note that Paul is wanting women to cover their heads. No, actually you decide he is commanding women to cover their heads. You, as a woman, reluctantly--and with much sorrow--open your hope chest and dust off Great Aunt Mabel's hat and wear it to the church-house the very next Sunday. Your mistake? Besides being in gross violation of the Fashion Laws, you violated Rule #2, and to an extent Rule #1 of the Six Rules of Interpretation. Men? Paul wasn't writing about you. If you insist on wearing the hat...well, you just wear that next Sunday and see how it plays out.

Say, by now you have jotted those six rules into one of the blank pages in your Bible, haven't you? This is why the various Bible publishers have gone to the extra expense and effort to place them there. [He's full of beans!] It is my belief that the blank pages in one's Bible are the greatest study help ever. Much can be written on those blank pages that will save the Bible student from reinventing the wheel again and again. On to the next example!

**Example #3:** You read First Corinthians chapter 11 and note (while wearing that monstrously outrageous hat of Aunt Mabel's from the preceding example) that Paul is wanting women to cover their heads. You, as a woman, decide while reading that this is <u>simply</u> and <u>only</u> a first century custom with absolutely <u>no application</u> for the church of today. You toss the hat and say, "So much for that hat!" Your mistake? You *mainly* violated step #2 of hermeneutical principles above. You did not look for a <u>lesson</u> or <u>directive</u> to Paul's recipients, a lesson that can be brought into the twenty-first century in either *type or kind*. If you are a man, and tossed the hat, we say, "Thank you, brother!"

**Example #4:** You read John chapters 13-17, paying special attention to the Holy Spirit promises. You look forward to the Spirit of God teaching you <u>all</u> things and bringing <u>all</u> things to your remembrance, guiding you into <u>all</u> truth and

The Bible Survival Manual:

whatever you ask of the Father, it will be given to you. You don't study for your licensing test, only to fail it. Subsequently you lose your job within thirty days. After losing your job, you wind up wandering the countryside destitute and in want. Your mistake? You violated rules #1 & #2 of the Six Rules of Interpretation. Probably rule #6, also.

By now, I hope that each reader is beginning to catch on to this thing called hermeneutics. Allow me to further expand on just why a correct hermeneutics is so vitally important. We will tramp familiar ground, but hopefully come away with a deeper understanding.

Give or take a few hundred years, the Bible was beginning to be penned down nearly four thousand years ago. The beginning of the Bible attempts to take the reader back to *In the Beginning*, yes, the beginning of all things! Two thousand years ago the Bible was closed. Some how, some way, God decided that everything we need here in the twenty-first century (and even a hundred or a thousand years from now) to be good, honest, sincere disciples of Christ, is contained within the pages of the Testaments, Old and New.

While your mind sinks in on that last paragraph, note again that the sacred text is written across a myriad of cultures--none of which match the one you and I are living in! The Bible isn't calling us to live in stone houses, busying ourselves everyday with trimming our olive oil lamps. Neither is it calling us to don our robes and ride donkeys about. In short, it isn't calling us back into any of the cultures we read about in the pages of the Bible, whether that be ancient Israel, Babylon, Palestine under Roman rule or a Hellenistic culture in the regions of Asia Minor. It is calling us to be something in our own culture--wherever that may be. That is hermeneutics!

Bringing the meaning of the text in such a way as to provide us with the correct overlay of the biblical principles in our day-to-day world. As has been noted, and you well know, mankind has quite often made a mess of that seemingly straightforward task. Failure to use all Bible tools correctly, then mucking the steps of hermeneutics, is one of the reasons we have such a splintering in Christendom today. Gander some of the following:

One group feels it is their sacred duty to cover the

communion table with a white cloth each quarter when they share the Lord's Supper. Another group shares it every week without all the fuss, however, all of their women have their heads covered. Another group thinks it is silly to have the women cover their heads. No, it is the men who should do so and they should pray while kneeling.

Yet another totally separate group baptizes candidates on fifth Sundays while a different group baptizes when the need arises. The first group believes immersion is a first work of grace while the second believes it is a milestone in salvation. A third group wonders what all the immersion fuss is, because they sprinkle any and everyone from babies to grandmothers. A fourth group thinks all three are washed up. Baptism is simply a Jewish ritual that doesn't apply to anyone today.

The list can go on and on, encompassing spiritual gifts, tithes and offerings, spiritual service of worship, music, a list of do's and don'ts that would choke a horse--all backed by a plethora of manuals and creeds! In short, we have done a horrible, horrendous, heinous job of hermeneutics. It is up to each one of us to carefully--and prayerfully--approach the Bible again with an open mind and an honest heart.

God is calling each disciple to be different from the world. How different? How would we describe this difference? This difference can be, of course, summed up in that which we have come to call the Greatest Commandments: loving God with all your everything, and loving your neighbor as yourself. That alone is so vastly different than the run-of-the-mill, work-a-day world, that it almost defies description! "So what?" one may ask, "Why is he bringing this up?" Keep reading.

We discussed bringing the meaning and lessons from the Bible, especially the difficulty of trying to transcend thousands of years and a plethora of cultures, into something that makes us different than our worldly surroundings. For a rule of thumb, if one delves into the pages of the Bible and comes up with a conclusion that is outrageous, something probably went wrong. Note, I didn't say a *conclusion that was different*, but outrageous! For an example of what is meant by outrageous, we only have to go to Ezekiel's life and ministry.

Take the time to read Ezekiel chapter four and note the absolute absurdity of the actions that God required the

The Bible Survival Manual:

prophet to undergo. Sure, God had His reasons for wanting the old prophet to do these strange and weird acts--seems that words alone weren't reaching God's people! However, this is not the norm and neither is it what God intends for us today. Now, let's concentrate on our conclusions in our day and age.

Again, we are to be different, not outrageous. I'm going to go way out here, but only in the interest of illustration. Suppose you read a few passages out of the Old Testament, then read the corresponding passages out of the New. These were rather lengthy passages, not some random verses pulled hither and yon out of their context. You think, ponder, re-read, take some time out, read further passages and your brain begins to crunch and whirl. Then you come up with a conclusion.

Next morning you awake to a new day. You don orange plaid pants, rubber overshoes, one of those red clown noses clamped onto your own nose, shave your head and go running all over town yelling, "Repent or perish!" while distributing little tracts and splashing 'holy water' on everyone you come in contact with. Now, as crazy as you think this is, I actually had to deal with a fellow in Virginia just like this. OK, sure, he didn't have the red rubber clown nose, but had everything else. Might as well have had the nose, for it couldn't have gotten any stranger.

After being kicked out of the local hospital for disrupting recuperating patients, especially in ICU and post-op, he was arrested downtown for assault with the holy water. How did a local preacher get involved? Easy, for it seems he had visited our church family a few Sundays prior and grabbed all of our tracts out of the display and was handing those out, complete with our name and address stamped on them while dousing folks with holy water!

But the illustration stands. God isn't calling us to be koo-koo nuts, just different. Koo-koo nuts turn the world off. Different will cause the world to at least pay attention--and some will be saved if we persevere. Why the long illustration? Because it comes down to interpretation based on what this book was attempting to guide.

If your interpretation of Scripture leads you to some outrageous conclusion, then it is time to check *both* your interpretation *and* your conclusion. It is time to painstakingly

## Mystifying to Manageable

go back over your Propprecids, check the context of every passage of Scripture making sure you aren't forcing an issue, rethink the Six Rules of Interpretation and lastly, review the steps of hermeneutics. This goes for the individual and the body corporate.

The what?! The local church. I am including straight-up some of the reptile handling that is going on across the nation every Sunday, along with the histrionics it entails. I am also including any wild and fantastic manifestation of Christianity that really doesn't enhance the cause of Christ. Not only does it not enhance our cause, it undermines it in front of the world. Remember the world? It is those folks that we're trying to save in the first place!

Koo-koo has spilled over into education, politics of all kinds, indeed almost every facet of any direction one can turn in today's world. Behind koo-koo is a warped view of Scripture, with more isogesis than one can beat with a long pole, ugly and up to ten feet in length. You don't be that. You be all that God would have you to be.

We will come back to this last sentence, but first I promised something way back there I feel I should make good on: a bit about the last book in the Bible, Revelation, with a few words thrown in about her sister book in the Old Testament: Daniel.

I saved these two books--and the discussion peraining to them--because it seems that a total misunderstanding of these two books of the Bible have a lot to do with hatching koo-koo nuts, especially in this country. A misunderstanding followed by a misapplication of these two books has done much to confuse the masses (or entertain them, depending...) at-large, and the church specifically.

Here we go. Keep an open mind. Use your Bible tools and knowledge.

The Bible Survival Manual:

# The Last Book

I don't want to make this section long. This book is nearing long enough as it is. Neither do I want to write a commentary on the book of Revelation, for I've already done that coupled with an exegesis of Daniel. Remember, I mentioned that there are not a few folks out there who strongly believe that there are only two books in the Bible: Daniel and Revelation.

No, they don't state such, but just listen to their sermons. Listen to their conversations. Read their literature. If you have a television hooked up to the outside world, tune into some of the religious programming on any Sunday night and witness what I'm talking about. Most of what they have to proclaim is fanciful at best.

During Daniel's time, the Jews were taken off of their land and into Babylonian captivity. For sure, they had a checkered past with folks coming into the Promised Land and sitting down hard on them for a time. The book of Judges will bear that out, however, this time they have been removed and their temple was dismembered and trampled. One can only wonder at what they were thinking for those seventy years: "Will we return? Will we ever have a temple again? Will our Holy City once again play host to feasts and sacrifices?"

Daniel's visions answer, "Yes," to all of the above questions, but he is given more information than that. He is also shown that someone called the Messiah will come and set up a Kingdom without end. Between the release from captivity and the coming of the Messiah, the home folks had better brace themselves for some not-so-pleasant times, the worst being the coming of Antiochus IV Epiphanes, who sorely desecrated the temple: the final act being the sacrifice of a swine on the Altar of God.

The Jews would have to put up with this madness several

years until the death of Epiphanes, and the cleansing and rededication of the temple in 164 BC--a holiday that is still celebrated by Jews today. This was the message of Daniel: it's bad, it is going to get worse, then there will come a glorious time, the church--*and there is never going to be a time when God is not on His Throne.*

Revelation closely follows both the theme and the make-up of Daniel. Out of the 404 verses in the book of Revelation, 378 of those verses are either a direct quote from, reference to, or allusion to an Old Testament verse. Many of those references, quotes and allusions are found in Daniel. And what might that theme be?

Acts chapter two had come and gone. The church, according to Acts, was growing by leaps and bounds in some places. Then some folks, mainly the Roman government, got their nose out of joint and began to persecute the saints. Sure, Satan was behind that and any other true persecution of God's people down through the ages (discounting self-inflicted stuff while wearing rubber clown noses), but it was wielded through the agency of man. Folks begin to be treated harshly for the sake of God. Folks began to get hurt. Folks began to die for the cause. Folks began to have questions. Revelation supplied those answers. This was the message of Revelation: it's bad, it is going to get worse, then there will come a glorious time, Heaven--*and there is never going to be a time when God is not on His Throne.*

That message looked familiar, didn't it?!

I'm not sure why folks like fantastic and surreal. I will leave that one up to the psychologists and sociologists to explain. I would ask that as you hear folks sitting around talking, with wide eyes of anticipation, about some fantastic time in the far away future (or next week, according to some) when a drunk, scarlet-clad whore will be riding a beast of the same color yelling blasphemies to the saints, that you take some thought to those who lived through the Roman persecution.

We like to talk in Sunday school about the time when our friends snubbed us at the watering hole at work because we are saints. We like to recount the time we were passed up for

The Bible Survival Manual:

a promotion because we are believers (never mind we weren't as qualified as the next fellow, or lacked having near enough education or experience!) and call that persecution. Instead, let's try this one on:

Wagers were made at the Roman circus. A mother and her infant-in-arms were placed in the arena with lions. The bet? Would the mother toss the infant to the lions and gain just a few more minutes of life, or would the maternal instinct be so tight that she would embrace her offspring, offering herself first? The scene played out, money exchanged hands, then another: would the father recant his faith before his entire family was doused in oil and set alight? It seemed, for a time, that there was no end to the sufferings that our brethren would have to go through. Would they have questions?

We shouldn't even need to ask that last one. However, it seems almost a slap in the face of those who went through all of those most horrible trials, receiving their robe and crown of life, when a significant portion of the church today clamors to hear, watch or read, the next installment of Biblical Fantasies Gone Wild. No, it is time to pull out your Bible tools and put them to work.

There, I've gone and written too much. Just keep one thing in mind, and that is God never wrote something to scare His kids. Yep, the Bible contains some scary stuff for non-believers, but not anything to scare and confuse His own. Anxiety is not an intended result for the Saints of God. Never.

Do your history. A wholly futuristic interpretation of the last six chapters of the book of Daniel, and the book of Revelation as a whole, is only about two-hundred years old. It came about on the heels of John Nelson Darby's writings about dispensationalism, and the seemingly fantastic gropings for wild interpretations that flared up in western thought (for reasons I have not yet fully explored) about the end of the eighteenth century and the first few decades of the next.

I'm not trying to start a war here. I couldn't, even if I wanted to, for that war has been started long ago by better folks than I. I'm simply trying to shed some additional light on Scriptural Interpretation. Something doesn't necessarily have to be, simply because some theologian said it had to be two-hundred years ago.

History, and the historical context, is important not just during Bible times, but in other times as well. We should be like the Berean disciples which Luke described in Acts chapter seventeen: searching to see if these things are so! It is that important. I believe, with this admonition, we can move into our final thoughts on Bible reading and study.

The Bible Survival Manual:

# Final Thoughts

Take the time to read John chapter fifteen, especially the first seventeen verses. Go ahead and open up and read it, even if you have a photographic memory and can quote it in the original Greek. I know, I know, it gets a little wordy and seemingly like Jesus is repeating Himself. It seems like it, because He is. It is an ancient Jewish way of teaching. There is a fancy name for it, but let's call it Rabbinical Droning! Say it, say it again, say it umpteen times. This was a way of stating the overall importance of something. Paul did it in places like the last half of Romans chapter seven. Our politicians do it today!

In our hurry-hurry, don't-got-a-whole-lotta-time life, we're a bit like Sergeant Friday from the Dragnet black-and-whites: *just the facts, ma'am.* In a Reader's Digest version of the first part of John chapter fifteen, we might be tempted to reduce the chapter to, "Do what Jesus says and you'll be fine!" But, Jesus had a point He wished to imbed into all those who would review His words down through the ages. He had more than 'do what I say' in mind.

He wanted us to *be* His words.

Yes, He is speaking to His twelve apostles (good catch!), but the 'anyone' of verse six expands this part of the teaching to us, today. It expands the teaching and promise to anyone who has gone before us in time, or will follow us, and clings to the teachings of God. And what is the outcome of those who abide in the Words of Christ?

We are forever joined to God, whether on Planet Here or the place we call Heaven. The design of Christianity is not to be a better friend and neighbor. We *will* be a better friend and neighbor, but that isn't the endpoint. The design of discipleship is not to be a better worker and a better parent. We will be a better worker and parent, but that isn't the endpoint. The endpoint is that we become a little more like Jesus today, than we were yesterday; tomorrow than today. Where can this start in the life of the heretofore untouched?

It can start with almost anything. The spark can begin with a kind word or a kind deed given by someone else who is imbedded with God. It may come through a song that will not leave someone's head, no matter how hard they try. The agency might be a sermon from the local preacher one Sunday, or a tract left on a stoop. Yes, and it just might come through a carefully worded fortune cookie! But that is the spark, the hook. The next phase is discipleship and subsequent maturity.

Here, we can drop songs and fortune cookies. Here, we must pick up the Word of God, the Bible, and carry on with it and it alone. Songs and sermons will have their place along the journey, but if we are to abide in the Words of Jesus and allow those Words to infiltrate our lives, we must be in contact with The Word. In a word: Bible reading.

One of my favorite passages is found in First Peter chapter one, at least the first eleven verses (so as to gain the context and not give birth to one of those pretexts!). Take the time to read it, noting that there are a few items in life such as moral excellence, self-control, brotherly kindness--and you can make your own list. Peter states in the 'negative' that if these are in our lives *and* increasing, we will be neither useless nor unfruitful in the true knowledge of Jesus, the Christ.

Why he didn't just say if those items were there, we *would* be fruitful and useful? I dunno. Ask him when you get there! But before you close out that little passage, go back to verse three and dissect it for a minute. Yes, God grants the life and godliness (or a 'godly life' if you are in the NIV or NIRV) to us, but look closely *how* He pulls that off: "through the true knowledge of Him..." (again, "through our knowledge of Him... if in the NIV).

Now, folks, as we close this little work, I'm wondering just how we get that true knowledge of God? I'll call that Bible reading and Bible study! See how that works? Ephesians 4:13 gives us about the same teaching: knowledge of the Son of God will move us into the mature category. Tingling Sunday services,

The Bible Survival Manual:

good Christian novels, heartfelt religious movies and a moving song on Christian radio have their moments, but knowledge of the Who, who tells us what goes much, much farther.

Amen!

Your Bible toolbox can be compared to any garage in Anytown, USA. Some garages do not have tools of any kind. Any time they need to fix something, the owners of that garage will end up going next door or across the street to borrow tools. More than likely, they will simply call on someone to come fix the leaky faucet for them.

Of course, this represents the person who has absolutely no Bible tools, whatsoever! In keeping with our illustration, this person is forced to either go to the religious powers (pastors, priests, preachers, whomever) and ask this or that question, or simply has no thoughts of their own. They rely solely on someone else to tell them what they should believe and think.

You don't be that person!

Another has tools, but they are random and haphazardly tossed into a canvass bag. One cannot see into that bag, therefore, the owner of that bag oftentimes forgets what tools they either have or don't have! Each time a problem comes up, they will have to empty the bag out onto the garage floor and sort through the mish-mash collection in front of them.

Invariably, they will--out of desperation--use a tool wrongly. A screwdriver will be used to pry; a 7/8 inch wrench will be used as a hammer; and a pair of channel lock pliers will be used as a 3/8 inch box wrench! Once the tip of the screwdriver is broken, and the 3/8 inch nut is rounded off, they will be forced to resort to the first fellow: either cross the street to borrow the correct tool or call the handy man.

You don't be that person!

A third person's garage has a toolbox. Inside that toolbox are actually tools. The problem with this person's toolbox is that it is woefully messy! It is unsorted. One doesn't necessarily

Mystifying to Manageable

need to dump out the tools on the garage floor each and every time a bicycle tire needs changing or the chain needs to be put back on, but the progress is slow because the right wrench for the job needs to be hunted in the various drawers and cubby holes of the toolbox.

In short, the person knows he possesses the right tool, but doesn't know exactly where it is at. As much time is spent finding the wrench as turning the wrench.

You don't be that person!

The fourth and final person has a fully stocked toolbox. Everything is neatly categorized and labeled: needle-nosed pliers in the second drawer, left hand side; ball-peen hammer in top compartment, middle tray; Phillips screwdriver set just to the right of the needle-nosed pliers!

Personally, I hate these kinds of guys and secretly want to superglue their toolbox drawers shut! I have a toolbox, but it looks more like the guy's in the preceding illustration. However, we're not talking about Black & Decker or Craftsman here--we're talking about our Biblical toolboxes.

You be this fourth person!

Don't loose heart. Don't give up. You may be the person who has...nothing...as far as tools right now. You might be carrying around a canvass bag with a few odds and ends in it. You might have the toolbox, but organization doesn't describe it in the least!

You CAN be this fourth fix-it person. It takes time to procure the necessary wrenches and screwdrivers needed to fill a complete and ready-to-go toolbox. You don't need to spend years at handy-man school or years as a journeyman (meaning seminary or Bible college) in order to both possess the right tools and know how to use them.

It takes time and practice. It takes prayer and determination backed by dedication. Once the toolbox is complete, then it is time to get that leather tool belt so that from time to time you can take selected tools out away from the main toolbox and go do work in a remote area, outside of your garage.

That is analogous to helping others, something we are called to do from time to time in the Bible.

---

There has been much in this book, however, compared to the Book of books, this is miniscule. This is only one man's attempt to break open the pages and allow the full meaning and intent to come flowing forth like the River of Life it is intended to be. The rest is up to you, the reader of God's Word.

And, don't lose heart. No, not with this book. I've already mentioned that way back in the foreword, just before our discussion about stupid questions. I mean don't lose heart with the Bible. Yes, some passages are difficult and will remain difficult throughout your lifetime. Others will be, not difficult to understand, but difficult to place into our lives due to culture, but especially our individual wills. We will simply just balk at changing our lives! Just keep after it.

Keep reading, praying, discussing with like-hearted, studying, praying, reading--and ever keep in mind that we are saved by grace through faith and not by any good deeds or accomplishments we have to our credit, for we have no credit with God. We seem to be the only ones who keep score.

God doesn't.

# About the Author

Interspersed among careers, degrees and certification in supervising oil and gas well drilling, law enforcement, clinical medicine and counseling, RF Pennington held full time ministry positions for twelve years after graduating from Sunset International Bible Institute and a Bachelors of Ministry from Theological University of America. For many years now RF has focused on house church ministries and writing. RF and Dee make their empty nest in El Paso, Texas.

Published writings include this book and *Allelon, Jude's Letter for Today's Path* and *A Healthy Thing Should Look Like This*.

CPSIA information can be obtained at www.ICGtesting.com
Printed in the USA
LVOW04s2116030914

402307LV00010B/95/P